ALL-TIME GREATEST ALABAMA SPORTS STORIES

Fire Ant Books

ALL-TIME GREATEST ALABAMA SPORTS STORIES

BENNY MARSHALL and FRIENDS

Edited by WENDELL GIVENS

The University of Alabama Press
Tuscaloosa

Typeface: Minion and Univers

∞

The paper on which this book is printed meets the minimum
requirements of American National Standard for Information
Science–Permanence of Paper for Printed Library Materials,
ANSI Z39.48-1984.

Library of Congress Cataloging-in-Publication Data

Marshall, Benny.
    All-time greatest Alabama sports stories / Benny Marshall and friends; edited by
Wendell Givens.
        p.   cm.
Includes index.
    ISBN 0-8173-5052-7 (pbk. : alk. paper)
    1. Sports—Alabama—Miscellanea. 2. Sports—Alabama—History. I. Givens, Wendell.
II. Title.
    GV584.A53 M37 2003
    796′.09761—dc21

                                                          2003006763

CONTENTS

Gifted Friend

WENDELL GIVENS

"BENNY PUT HIS ARMS AROUND YOU with his words and took you along wherever he went," wrote the *Tampa Tribune*'s Tom McEwen of his friend Benny Marshall of the *Birmingham News*.

Nashville Banner executive and sports editor Fred Russell said of Marshall, "He had a feel for writing that few men possess."

Many of the sports figures Marshall wrote about felt the same. One of his longtime friends, Alabama coach Paul Bryant, commented, "He had the God-given ability to put things down on paper that could have you chuckling one minute and crying the next."

I tagged along as editor of Benny's *Winning Isn't Everything*, a book of Bryant portraits that reflected the respect between coach and writer. My editing was little more than negotiating with a printer; Marshall needed little editing.

Delighted with the response to his Bryant book, a quick sellout, Benny sauntered by one day and asked if I had a suggestion for a second book. I proposed that he write a collection of Alabama's all-time great sports events, many of which he had covered; the others I knew he could reconstruct from *Birmingham News* and *Age-Herald* back issues.

He agreed, and then and there Benny began recalling some of the obvious greats (or "grands," as we decided to entitle them): Alabama's Dixie Howell and Don Hutson in the 1935 Rose Bowl, the Monk Gafford–led Auburn upset of Georgia (with star backs Sinkwich and Trippi) in 1942, Willie Mays's superb catch in the 1954 World Series, blind golf champion Charley Boswell's great courage, and—well, as Benny noted in his foreword—*20 Grand* just as easily could have been *40 Grand*.

Through the years, Marshall, who at age seventeen had been a Howard College senior, won uncounted sports-writing awards, visited the White House with one of Coach Bryant's national championship Alabama teams, and with his wife, Ruth, shared the joy of rearing four bright children: David, Phillip, Ellen, and Matthew.

Having worked closely with Benny on the *Age-Herald* and later the *Birmingham News,* I can attest to his versatility. He didn't just turn out a daily sports column, he was a most-valuable-player type. He put together and supervised one of the finest sports department staffs in the land; for years he planned, laid out, and helped edit the daily *News* sports section, all the while inspiring veteran and rookie writers.

Unknown to some of his friends, Marshall suffered at times from depression in his later years. Then, after two heart attacks further hampered his cherished career, in September 1969 he ended his life.

Sixteen chapters from Marshall's *20 Grand* make up the bulk of this book. All but one of the authors of the additional ten chapters had worked closely with Benny. The exception is his son Phillip, who was too young at the time to be on his father's staff but later became a talented sportswriter for the *Huntsville Times.*

Those of us who have added chapters to Marshall's original *20 Grand* hope our efforts help in a small way to preserve our friend's very special way with words.

ALL-TIME
GREATEST
ALABAMA
SPORTS
STORIES

1

September Memory

September 16, 1931

I WAS VERY YOUNG. IT WAS mid-September and hot, I remember, and my father came home near dark on the streetcar that made its stop two houses down the street.

His flat straw hat was shoved back on his head, meaning that he felt good and jaunty about something, and he had the late edition of the *Birmingham News* in the pocket of his coat. This was the edition that came out all in pink, rivaling the *Birmingham Post,* which came in green. He was singing "Take Me Out to the Ball Game." What his voice lacked in tone it made up for in enthusiasm. A man who had a song to sing should sing it—that was the way he felt about it when he felt good.

"You left work," said my mother. Her voice was faintly accusing, for the hard times were closing in, and a man with a family shouldn't just walk off from a day's work. If he heard her he gave no sign, for he had news for two little boys who knew that this was the day old Ray Caldwell would pitch against young Dizzy Dean at Rickwood Field, home of the Birmingham Barons.

My father was not alone on September 16, 1931, in Birmingham.

Practically everyone had left work, and the bosses knew what for, but no one seemed really to care. The bosses left work too.

A crowd of 20,074 had overflowed the baseball park in Birmingham's West End for the first game of the 1931 Dixie Series between the Southern League champion Barons and Texas League champion Houston. It got to be a joke around town in the years after, when this game my father had gone to see was being paid proper homage, that if everyone had seen it who said he saw it, all the ballparks in the Southern League wouldn't have held the crowd.

"You should've seen it," my father said, as if he didn't know that any schoolboy chained to his desk that day almost would have given his catcher's mitt for a place in the mob that boarded the open-air trolleys and went whooping and laughing to the magnificence of the stadium A. H. (Rick) Woodward had built and named for himself.

"You should've seen that Caldwell, and that Dean. Oh, you should've seen it."

Then, "What?" almost resenting the interruption of a big moment he had brought home. "Sure the Barons won. They won 1 to 0. Caldwell beat him."

Maybe today, in what surely is another century, that might not sound like much. The Class A team from Birmingham beat the Class A team from Texas, but this was another time that you must understand if you would know how magnificent the news was that came home to houses all over the city that afternoon.

From April to September, nothing was bigger in the cities of the Southern League than the baseball teams that played in them. The major leagues were a million miles away, and there was no television to show the outlanders that Babe Ruth could look foolish striking out too, just like Jiggy Black or Woodley Abernathy.

At Birmingham, Little Rock, Memphis, Chattanooga, New Orleans, Atlanta, Knoxville, and Nashville, baseball teams were still a mixture of fading stars, down from the majors, and youngsters on the way up. The players were swashbuckling citizens whose cheeks always bulged from a cud of Brown Mule or Apple Sun cured, and sometimes Beechnut, though this was too sweet a chewing tobacco for the real he-man ballplayer.

They played their games in the afternoon, and occasionally stories were heard of other kinds of games played in the night, but they weren't important unless the team was losing. No local hero could figure to walk the block on Second Avenue downtown from Twentieth Street to Nineteenth without a dozen people pointing him out and a half-dozen stopping to ask him about yesterday's game. Kids who were fortunate enough to have a ballplayer move into their neighborhood in the summer knew the minute he left in the morning, exactly when he came home in the afternoon, and if his wife made him go to the grocery store. Secretly, they wished they could have been his kids.

Around Birmingham, all the ball fans had a great summer in 1931. Johnny Dobbs had gone on to manage Atlanta, and Clyde Milan ran the team for the first time. He had Caldwell, who had pitched all around the majors and was now forty-three; and Bob Hasty and Jimmy Walkup, also veterans, who knew how to pitch. He had a local hero, Billy Bancroft, at second base, and another, Woodley Abernathy, in center field. The names of the famous linger still, strong in my memory of the warm months of 1931: Bill Eisemann, the catcher; Shine Cortazzo, the shortstop; Art Weiss, the left fielder; Joe Prerost, in right field. They won the Southern League pennant by ten and a half games over Little Rock, a runaway like the Southern League hadn't seen since 1924 when Memphis finished nine and a half ahead of second-place Atlanta.

Rumblings were coming from Texas, where Houston had set a new Texas League attendance record by drawing more than 230,000 fans while winning the pennant. Houston had Ducky Medwick on his way to the Cardinals, and others, but mostly what Houston had was Jerome H. Dean, age twenty, who it was said could throw as hard as Walter Johnson in his prime.

It would be Dean, the kid, against Caldwell, the old guy, in the first game for the championship of Dixie, and Dean could help with the setting of a stage. He sent boastful challenges ahead of him. Every day for a week beforehand Dizzy Dean was being quoted in the papers. The temperature of Birmingham rose with every edition. Civic pride was insulted. Birmingham would show *him*. No telling how many extra tickets Dizzy sold for the Texas League and the Southern League. He was why the town was on its ear when the morning of September 16 arrived, the day of the start of the Dixie Series.

Billy Bancroft remembers that he got up as usual at about 8 or 8:30, and pretty young Mrs. Bancroft, who had been Claudie Mae Hoover, his Woodlawn High School and Howard College sweetheart, gave him bacon and eggs and biscuits for breakfast. They talked about the ball game, but not for long, because the Birmingham second baseman, a small ball of fire who stood about five feet-six and weighed no more than 145, had to be at the park for the meeting Manager Milan had called for 10 A.M.

This day was Dean's and Caldwell's, but it also would be Billy Bancroft's day before it was over triumphantly for Birmingham.

Billy, who had been a twenty-five-year-old Southern League rookie in 1930 as Birmingham's utilityman after getting a thousand dollars for signing with the Barons and going to the lower minors in 1929, drove his Model A Ford roadster in on First Avenue, through town, cut across to Third Avenue, and made the meeting early. Bancroft was a hustler who'd never be late to anything. He played baseball that way, as he'd played football, too, for Howard.

Already the fans were heading toward the park, and Rick Woodward, the owner, and Billy West, who ran the team, could feel it. This was going to be the greatest ever. The Birmingham Electric Company was ready with extra streetcars and the open-air trailers hitched on behind. Fans doted on these, and soon they were coming from downtown in a great rush. This was *their* team, and Dizzy Dean had talked too much. Somehow, honor must be preserved, an upstart must be put in his place. That's how the fans felt, and they came on and on and on until they'd filled all the grandstand seats and the bleachers. They lined the foul lines and the outer reaches of the outfield. Nothing in Birmingham's history had ever brought such a crowd together,

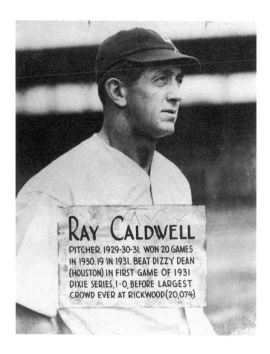

RAY CALDWELL
PITCHER. 1929-30-31. WON 20 GAMES
IN 1930. 19 IN 1931. BEAT DIZZY DEAN
(HOUSTON) IN FIRST GAME OF 1931
DIXIE SERIES, 1-0, BEFORE LARGEST
CROWD EVER AT RICKWOOD (20,074).

Ray Caldwell. (Courtesy *Birmingham News*)

not even when Charles A. Lindbergh flew in the *Spirit of St. Louis* that time.

So the duel began. Dean could knock a bat out of a hitter's hand. Caldwell couldn't break a pane of glass. Ray was in his twenty-third season of pitching baseball for a living, and all the spring of youth was gone from his arm. But he had the know-how of the twenty-three years working for him, and he could throw the ball where he wanted it to go.

The pattern truly was classic. Strength of youth versus the guile of years, and, now and then, the race does not go to the swiftest. Sometimes, the turtle does get there ahead of the rabbit. If the rabbit wins, there's no story. If Dizzy Dean had won, who'd have remembered?

They went scorelessly from the start, Caldwell in a jam now and then, Dean moving easily along. Dizzy gave up one hit over the first six innings of zero, zero, and more zero. He wasn't striking them out as he was supposed to, but no one was getting on base. Houston had

Dizzy Dean. (Courtesy *Birmingham News*)

two men on in the first, but Abernathy took a hit away from Medwick in right-center. Bancroft made a great play, later, going behind the bag to field Guy Sturdy's smash with his bare hand and throw him out. When Caldwell got the game's first strikeout in the sixth, the crowd roared approval, and it turned out that the Birmingham pitcher had saved something. He was getting stronger now, tougher to hit.

Medwick led the sixth with a single, the seventh hit off Caldwell, and that was that for Houston. Caldwell would not give up another. He was in command. In the seventh, the old pitcher fumbled a grounder and that put a runner on, but Ray's big curve ball kept him clear of danger. A hit and a walk put two on for Birmingham with two out in the seventh, but nothing came of it. Could this go on forever? The crowd almost was quiet, waiting, ready to explode, needing the lighting of the fuse.

Now, the eighth inning. Houston up. Houston out on two strikeouts and a pop-up to Zach Taylor. Two up, two out in the Birming-

Shine Cortazzo (*left*), Billy Bancroft, and admirers.
(Courtesy *Birmingham News*)

ham half, then Taylor, the catcher, put a two-strike single into right field. Now Caldwell was at bat. A pinch hitter? Milan never gave it a thought. He let Caldwell hit, and Caldwell got a single over second. Taylor ran to third, and Billy Bancroft came toward the plate. Milan hurried down from the third-base coaching box to say nothing more than, "C'mon kid. Just one hit wins this ball game."

Bancroft moved in, close to the plate, crowding it, daring Dean. He swung at a fastball strike. Another strike was called. It was a fastball, too, Billy Bancroft would remember for all the years of his life. Then, young Diz made a mistake.

"He threw a curve ball," Bancroft said. "It hung up there, or something. It wasn't a very good curve ball. I guess he thought he was going to fool me, or maybe he thought he would waste it."

If that was the thought, it was in error. Bancroft swung with all the strength in his short, solid frame, and his drive was over third base, into left field, a shot down the line in spacious Rickwood that might have been a triple, or maybe a home run, because Billy the Kid could fly around the bases. But the ball caromed into the stands for a ground-rule double. It didn't matter. Taylor was home with the only run Caldwell would need. He took the ninth with a strikeout and two ground balls to Pete Susko at first, and the game that everyone would swear ten or twenty years later they'd seen was Birmingham's.

Dean hadn't struck out a man. Caldwell had struck out five. Dean would come back to win a later game as the series went the limit to seven, then Birmingham nailed him again with Caldwell relieving Bob Hasty to save the day and the winner's share of almost a thousand dollars.

Dizzy's greatest years were still ahead, of course. Caldwell was at the end of the road, and he wouldn't win again. Another season and he'd dropped from sight as Dean went to work winning and talking the same way, still, for the St. Louis Cardinals.

Caldwell wouldn't forget. Neither, for that matter, would Dean through his playing time and through radio and telecasting success that followed when he settled down in Wiggins, Mississippi.

At the time of this writing Bancroft was boys adviser at Woodlawn High School. He quit baseball in 1935 to head-coach Howard football, and his first team tied Alabama 7–7, which is another story. Caldwell died in 1966, a very old man, and the notices on the wires spoke only of his big-league years—where the right-handed pitcher had been and what he'd done. They didn't know, or maybe they'd forgotten, or perhaps it didn't matter, that he had beaten Dizzy Dean.

Long since, my father is dead, and the other little boy died at Iwo Jima in World War II. I think now that there had to be many fathers in Birmingham who left work, then came home on September 16, 1931, with hats pushed back, with songs in the voices that lighted the eyes of their sons because Ray Caldwell had won, and this surely was the happiest day anyone ever had known, anywhere. That's the way it was with baseball then.

2

Tiger Trap

November 21, 1942

COLUMBUS, GEORGIA, ON NOVEMBER 21, 1942, was any town nearby an Army establishment: overcrowded, raucous, full of infantry soldiers from nearby Fort Benning on their way to war. It was a frantic time, an eat, drink, and be merry time. The joints across the river in Phenix City never closed. There were girls and gambling, music and bright lights, and you took your fun where you found it because the tomorrows were running out.

American troops were driving against the Japanese on Guadalcanal, and Britain's fabulous Eighth Army was chasing Marshal Rommel across the desert. Allied troops were closing in on Tunis and Bizerte in North Africa. At Pearl Harbor, Captain Eddie Rickenbacker was telling of his rescue after twenty-two days lost at sea when an Army plane went down. There were twenty-seven shopping days until Christmas.

In Columbus there was a football game to be played by young men who themselves would be gone to war in another year. The man was lucky who could get a ticket to squeeze into one of the eighteen thousand seats in Columbus's Memorial Stadium, scene then and for many years after of the Auburn-Georgia game. This was an occasion, a party lasting all week for Georgians, and the Ralston Hotel echoed, still, the merriment of the night before when Jack Meagher put his Auburn squad on the train Saturday morning for the quick ride over to Columbus. This time the students didn't impede progress. They had been known in the past to soap the tracks to a point where train wheels did nothing except spin. It was the kind of thing happy college kids did back then.

At the University of Georgia they remember 1942 as the football season when Frank Sinkwich and Charlie Trippi ran wild from the same backfield and Wally Butts took them to the Rose Bowl where the Bulldogs did UCLA in. Georgia remembers this, and that this team came magnificently off the floor in the fourth quarter to whip Alabama 21–10, massacred Florida 72–0, and insulted Georgia Tech 34–0. Oh, they had a lot of fun with football that year at Georgia, and Wally surely was the greatest football coach in the world.

In 1942, football wasn't being such a much for Auburn. The Florida team that Georgia mangled was a team able to put down Jack Meagher's Tigers 6–0. A low spot there, and there were others. High spots too, but not many. Auburn was up, down, in, out, but nothing really to get worked up about for most of that autumn. The War Eagles were loud, but more in defiance than in joy. They're our boys, they try hard, and maybe next week . . .

Georgia won ten games on the happy road to the Rose Bowl, but Georgia lost one.

On that November 21 at Columbus, Auburn's football team bound for nowhere took Georgia's greatest team apart 27–13 in what still must be recorded as one of the most stunning football upsets of all time.

Phenix City bookmakers anticipated a harvest. An Auburn man with money to bet could get from twenty-seven to thirty-seven points the morning of the game. Georgia had opened slowly, 7–6 over Kentucky, but then the Bulldogs had dusted off Jacksonville Naval Air Station 14–0, Furman 40–7, Mississippi 48–13, Tulane 40–0, Cincinnati 35–13, then Alabama, then Florida and Chattanooga 40–0, leading up to the tenth game of an eleven-game season. Auburn, meanwhile, had been erratic. The Tigers beat little Chattanooga 20–7, then lost to Georgia Tech 15–0. They whipped Tulane 27–13, then lost to Florida 6–0. They tied Georgetown 6–6, beat Villanova 14–6, and lost to Mississippi State 6–0 on a rainy day in Birmingham. Georgia Navy Pre-Flight was much too much for Auburn, 41–14, but on the Saturday before Georgia there was a sign many didn't see. Underdog Auburn decked Louisiana State 25–7 at Legion Field, and Auburn was about to have a surprise for the Bulldogs.

Monday of the week of the renewal of the oldest college football rivalry in the South had found Meagher paying a call on Bill Alexander, the great Georgia Tech coach. Meagher's plans now included a new wrinkle, an old formation making a comeback. There would be four T-formation plays in the Tiger arsenal for the Bulldogs. Joe Eddins of Birmingham, a fine senior tackle who had suffered through a 14–13 loss to Georgia in 1940 and a 7–0 Bulldog victory in 1941, remembers that the plays were numbered "Sixty-one, sixty-two, sixty-three, and sixty-four." They were all straight handoffs, quick plays inside the tackles that involved a new kind of blocking. "Shadow blocking," Coach Meagher called it.

If Coach Meagher, a soft-voiced, dry-funny product of the Notre Dame school of inspirational leadership, thought that this was the thing to do, no man on his football squad would think otherwise. Jack Meagher's players thought then, and still do, that he must have been a coaching genius. He was never overloaded with football-playing talent, but he taught blocking and he taught tackling, and a boy wanted to play all he could when Jack Meagher sent him out with a job to do. Meagher practically never raised his voice, never swore, but his eyes could bore a hole.

There would be T for the offense, brand new, and no Georgia scouting report could have a hint of it. Defensively, too, Meagher varied his preparation. Auburn linemen would take a step left before they charged, or a step right. Tackles would fade back from time to time, covering for the ends who would crash. This was the plan Monk Gafford, Jim Reynolds, Zack Jenkins, Captain Vic Costellos, Jack Cornelius, Eddins, Fagan Canzoneri, Charlie Finney, Aubrey Clayton, Jim McClurkin, Babe Gendusa, Louis Chateau, Clarence Harkins, and fellow Tigers would execute. One Auburn halfback was a little uncertain about the new formation and the four plays off it which would be most of Auburn's offense. He had them written on a slip of paper, tucked inside his pants.

Thus was the stage set for a game that would stir the usually non-excitable Bob Phillips to soar away on for the *Birmingham News* on the Sunday morning after: "How the mighty have fallen . . . "

The game began as it was expected to begin, with big Georgia on the move. George Poschner hauled the kickoff out twenty-five yards to the Bulldog forty-five yard line, and Butts's bowl-bound forces wheeled away to a touchdown. Sinkwich had runs of thirteen and eight yards along the way. The all-American passed to Van Davis for fourteen, and presently Georgia was on the Auburn two. Pass interference had been called there when Poschner stumbled, going after a Sinkwich pitch. Flat-footed Frankie busted across from the two. Lee Costa missed the try for point, but it seemed hardly to matter. That's the way things turned out, though not in the manner expected at this juncture.

Sinkwich, who did everything except carry the water bucket, kicked off over the goal. Auburn lined up in the T on first down at its twenty, and Auburn was about to be off to the races.

Clayton ran five yards and Reynolds ten off quick openers. Gafford, whose greatness was never recognized sufficiently in newspapers and other places, and maybe not by some latter-day Tiger fans, ripped ten yards from the Bulldogs, then thirty-four on a brilliant run to the Georgia thirteen. Reynolds and Gafford alternated, going to first down on the two, and Reynolds charged over the goal. Chateau kicked the seventh point and Auburn had the lead for good, though the first quarter was not over.

At the half it was 14–6. The Tigers moved out from their forty-four yard line after a fifteen-yard penalty against Georgia for roughing Harkins on a punt return. Zack Jenkins took off for fourteen yards, then was away for twenty-two on a pitchout from Clayton. Reynolds charged seven yards to the eight, got only two yards on two more tries against fierce Georgia resistance, then Clayton went to first down on the three. This was tough going, but the Tigers weren't stopping. Reynolds made a yard. Clayton lost a yard when he fumbled and Gafford, the Fort Deposit firebrand, recovered. Clayton tried a pass to Clarence Grimmett but missed. Fourth down now, and Gafford got the call. For a fraction of a second the Bulldog appeared to have stopped his lunge for the end zone, but what modern coaches call "second effort" was second nature to Monk Gafford. He kept on keeping on for three yards and the second Auburn touchdown. Chateau kicked the fourteenth point.

They fought through a scoreless third quarter with neither side able to get moving, but early in the fourth period Gafford hauled a Sinkwich punt twenty-nine yards to Georgia's nineteen. Reynolds and Jenkins made first down, just made it, on the nine. Gendusa bucked four yards to the five. Reynolds made one yard, Gafford three, then it was Reynolds going in, with a yard to spare. Chateau missed and it was a quite shocking 20–6.

There was still hope for Georgia, and time, when three penalties drove the Tigers back to their one yard line on their next possession. Gafford's run from the twenty-three to midfield was nullified by a holding penalty. Two plays later a penalty for unsportsmanlike conduct brought a Gendusa punt from the one. It went out only twenty-five yards, and on third down from the thirty-four, Sinkwich threw a touchdown to Lamar Davis. On first down, Davis had dropped one. On second down, Grimmett and Eddins had thrown Sinkwich for a nine-yard loss, but Davis didn't miss the third-downer, and when Costa converted, Georgia trailed 20–13 with seven minutes to play.

Georgia couldn't get much done in that time, but Auburn could. The Tigers went from their thirty-four yard line after the kickoff to Georgia's sixteen before losing the ball, and they had controlled it for

Monk Gafford high-steps toward the Georgia goal as a Tiger trap springs
shut. (Courtesy Auburn University)

five precious minutes. Two minutes remained when Sinkwich went
back for his last desperate effort to pull it out of the fire. Gafford
knocked down his first pass. A second try ended up an eleven-yard
loss. On third down the Tigers ganged Sinkwich in the end zone, he
fumbled, and Fagan Canzoneri leaped on the ball for a touchdown.
Chateau's kick was true, and Georgia had been whipped badly.

How badly? Well, 27–13, 335 yards rushing to 37. Only in the air
could Georgia go at all. Sinkwich passed for 190 yards. The Tigers
tried only five passes and completed none. One was intercepted at
the one-yard line to cut off a threat, and all afternoon long it was
Auburn threatening to break out . . . after a sixty-one-yard Gafford
punt return, after a thirty-five-yard Jenkins gallop, after a nineteen-
yard Gafford return setting up a drive from midfield to the Georgia

twenty-seven, on a march from their thirty-five near the first half's end to the Georgia twelve before a Van Davis interception stopped that. If stunned Georgia hadn't kept its gallantry, the Bulldogs would have suffered even greater indignity.

Joe Eddins's clearest recollection of the autumn afternoon still is of the coach, Jack Meagher, standing on the sidelines at the happiest moment of his football career. He had called his regulars in with a little while to play, letting the substitutes finish up, and as they ran from the field they found him with good, honest, honorable tears rolling from the intense eyes, down the craggy face, and he looked at them and could find no words to tell them. He didn't need the words. The Auburn football players knew, and some of them cried, too, before all the laughing began. Not even the fire that had come from the potbellied stove in the dressing room and left clothes scorching could stop the laughing.

After Saturday's sweat and tears, after Sunday's rejoicing, always there is Monday. Meagher gathered his squad around him two days after Georgia had been hammered. They would have the day off, but he wanted a word, and they sat on the grass at his feet and listened when he told them, "The whole nation knows who you are now, but they'll think this was nothing except a fluke if we don't beat Clemson, and if we don't make it impressive."

The next Saturday, which was the last Saturday, Auburn handled Clemson 41–13, and that made the record for the year six wins, four losses, and a tie. Meagher had coached his last Auburn team. He went away to the Marines, and when the school returned to football in 1944, Carl Voyles was given the head job. Meagher's old boys like the knowledge that the last three they gave him were the very best: 25–7 over Louisiana State, 27–13 over Georgia, 41–13 over Clemson; these three, and the greatest of these was Georgia on the day the Bulldogs were introduced to T, Tiger style.

3

Howell to Hutson to History

January 1, 1935

Once upon a time, there was a football game called the Rose Bowl game, played in a stadium called the Rose Bowl in Pasadena, California.

There still is a Rose Bowl, squatting down beneath the mountains that go up as high as snow, and from the top of the mountain the Rose Bowl must look very small, though more than a hundred thousand go on New Year's Day every year to see football teams from the Pacific Coast and teams from the Big Ten play. It's a very big place for football, and a very big game.

But this isn't the once-upon-a-time Rose Bowl.

The once-upon-a-time Rose Bowl was the only thing of its kind, and for a college football team to go there and play the best of the West was the ultimate, the grandest of prizes. No one could aspire to more. Little boys playing football in backyards daydreamed themselves in the Rose Bowl, and part of it was that the entire country would be watching the glory the next week in newsreels in movie houses everywhere. Grantland Rice would write about it.

From almost anywhere, it was a week's ride on the train to the Rose

Bowl, with stops along the way to practice, and Hollywood waiting. A star halfback would have his picture taken with beautiful movie stars, and everyone back home would know that he stood at least ten feet tall. He was coast-to-coast, Jim Thorpe young again, or later, perhaps, Red Grange.

It was January 1, 1926, when Alabamians first discovered that the Rose Bowl wasn't an impossible dream. Wallace Wade took Pooley Hubert, Johnny Mack Brown (who would stay and become a movie star), and their bunch, which had won nine games and allowed only one touchdown in the 1925 season. They beat Washington 20–19, and now the whole United States of football knew about Southern football in general, the Alabama brand most specifically.

California knew a good thing. After another undefeated Alabama season in 1926, back went the Tide to the Rose Bowl, this time to play Stanford, and that was a 7–7 tie. Wade went again to conquer Washington State 24–0, on January 1, 1931, after they had been undefeated in the 1930 season, also.

Then came Frank Thomas, a Knute Rockne pupil from Notre Dame, a chunky, round-faced man who had been George Gipp's best college friend before that Fighting Irish immortal died. Thomas had been Rockne's regular quarterback in 1921 and 1922, then went to Georgia as an assistant for two years, spent three years head-coaching Chattanooga, went back to Georgia to assist Harry Mehre one year, then Dr. Mike Denny hired him for Alabama as Wade went on to Duke.

Now, Alabama would run from Rockne's Notre Dame box, and Thomas came on strongly, but even a sixteen-hours-a-day work schedule for himself couldn't prevent a 25–0 loss to Tennessee in 1931, the one defeat of his first season, and in his second, a 7–3 defeat by Tennessee and a 6–0 loss to Georgia Tech. There was a 0–0 tie with Ole Miss and a 2–0 defeat by Fordham in 1933, and the Rose Bowl didn't know where Alabama lived. Frank Thomas knew, too, that inevitably what he had accomplished must be compared with what Wade had done before him.

Then came 1934. A skinny onetime end from Hartford, Alabama, named Millard (Dixie) Howell had become the regular left halfback, the triple-threat position in the Notre Dame attack. Dixie Howell had gotten the job when Joe Riley was hurt, and his eighty-two-yard touchdown run had beaten Vanderbilt 7–0 in the last game of 1933.

Also there was an end named Paul Bryant, who was called Bear, and a fellow Arkansan, Don Hutson, at the other end. Riley Smith was the blocking back (quarterback), Bill Lee an all-American tackle. Frank Thomas was about to find out about the Rose Bowl, where Wade went three times, where Thomas had never been with an Alabama team.

The 1934 Crimson Tide, getting stronger as it went, had knocked over eight in a row, Tennessee included, when November 29 of that year brought Vanderbilt to Birmingham for the last game. Thomas called the starting team together, and he had a telegram in his hand. He read it to them. "If you win, where can we contact you immediately after the game?" The wire was signed, "Al Masters, Stanford University." Stanford meant the Rose Bowl.

Paul Bryant, who would take Alabama teams to bowls upon top of bowls after he became Alabama's coach in 1958, can hear it still, the beautiful music the band was blaring as he came running off Legion Field that Saturday afternoon with two minutes to play and Alabama ahead 34–0.

Alabama's band played "California, Here We Come!"

Thirty-six-year-old Frank Thomas had made it. The invitation and acceptance were Saturday-night business, big in the Sunday-morning papers. Alabama would play Stanford on January 1, 1935, in the Rose Bowl. The choice wasn't particularly popular. Coast fans had wanted Minnesota to come play Stanford's great team, which now was accused of hunting up a soft touch. Stanford wanted Alabama, it was being said, because Stanford knew that Alabama, despite its perfect record, would be a sure win for Stanford.

Thomas, master psychologist, would not let his players forget the slights, printed and spoken, as they practiced at Tuscaloosa, as they rode the train west, finally, toward great adventure. The travel pattern was the same as usual, except Thomas provided a shrewd touch for the special train. He put his players on the cars up front, and then came the baggage cars, while partying Crimson Tide supporters, parents, and sweethearts came in the back. There was a barrier. Thomas wanted his football team thinking nothing but football.

Mary Harmon Black of Troy, Alabama, a campus beauty who would become Mrs. Paul Bryant, went in one of the cars on the back. She would have preferred spending more time with her tall, handsome, football-hero sweetheart, but it might have been good training for a young lady about to spend her life with the game that recognizes no diversions. When there is a game to be played, there is nothing but the game. This, too, was part of what Frank Thomas taught Paul Bryant.

Alabama still was the "nobody" team when New Year's Day arrived, celebrated noisily at the Huntingdon Hotel where Alabama players and many fans had lived the last days before the big show that was to bring more than eighty-five thousand—a record crowd—to the Rose Bowl. Obviously, many Stanfords wanted in on the feasting.

Mary Harmon Black was a sponsor, which meant she got to sit in a front-row box seat because sponsors were not paraded out for all to see in those days. The front-row box seat meant that she couldn't see much of what was happening, but it wasn't pretty to watch at first, anyway.

There was an Alabama fumble. Stanford got it. Stanford was stopped. Alabama fumbled again, and the Indians covered this one on the Alabama twenty-five. Presently, the great Bobby Grayson was slamming the final yard to a touchdown. Stanford led 7–0. Had the rout begun? As a matter of fact, it had not. Will Rogers's laughing piece on the front page of the *Birmingham News* the next day said, "That touchdown was like holding up a picture of Sherman's March to the Sea in front of the Alabama boys."

They were well into the second quarter when Dixie Howell hauled a punt back twenty-five yards and Alabama saw the door opened.

Howell passed to Hutson for seventeen yards, to Jimmy Angelich for eleven. An end-around with Bryant carrying lost five yards, but Howell was right back with a pass to Bryant that went to the five, and Howell ran it in. Smith missed his extra-point kick, leaving the Crimson Tide behind 7–6, but this was only a momentary setback.

For reasons best known to itself, lost back in the years, Stanford chose to kick off after the touchdown, daring revved-up Alabama. The decision was a mistake. From their twenty yard line, after the kickoff was out of the end zone, Alabama swarmed upfield again.

Hutson caught a twenty-five-yard pass from Howell, and Bryant grabbed a seventeen-yarder on the way to the five yard line. Stopped there, Alabama called on Smith for a field goal and he delivered. The Tide led 9–7, and the fun really was just beginning for Frank Thomas's team and for the twenty-five hundred rooters from the South who had come out of hiding in the great crowd and would not be silent again.

Once more, Stanford kicked off. Howell returned twenty yards to Alabama's twenty-five yard line. Angelich ran seven, then on third down, from punt formation, Dixie Howell of Hartford, Alabama, broke the back of the resistance. Howell headed between end and tackle, then swung wide, and Stanford's defense had come in too far, too soon. The Indians were set up perfectly for the blockers hammering ahead of the runner.

Bill Lee got a man, Joe Demyanovich another, and Kay Francis, the center, a third. Bryant took care of the Stanford left tackle, Angelich removed the linebacker, and Smith the defensive half back over there. Howell was beyond the line, cutting back to the middle, and he needed one more block. Hutson gave it to him, and Howell was one-on-one with the safetyman. Howell one-on-one should have been against the law. The slim-jim with the loose-jointed, deceptive gait faked the safetyman out of his shoes, and nothing was ahead but the goal line. Howell coasted in, turning to thumb his nose at the closest pursuers as he went across at the end of a sixty-eight-yard run. Smith kicked, and it was 16–7.

Alabama's famed Rose Bowl battery, Howell and Hutson, back in Tuscaloosa. (Courtesy *Birmingham News*)

Howell came out of the game, suffering from severe stomach cramps, and Joe Riley had his chance, which he promptly put to good advantage. Smith's interception of a pass on the Alabama forty-six stopped Stanford after the kickoff, Stanford having decided it was better to receive than to give. With eight seconds remaining in the half, Riley threw at Hutson on the fourteen. The catch was spectacular, and Hutson ran in to score. Smith's kick missed, but it had been a twenty-two-point quarter, turning the game completely over.

Stanford struck back in the third quarter, driving sixty-seven yards after the kickoff, scoring from the twelve on a reverse. It was 22–13 after the placement try went wide, but Stanford could hope again. The Indians drove again, too, late in the quarter until Francis's interception stopped them on the Alabama twenty-six.

Alabama was on the Stanford forty-five as the last quarter began, lost fifteen on a holding penalty, but got it all back right away with room to spare. From his forty, Howell lofted another pass to Hutson, who took the ball on Stanford's thirty and kept going. No one ever would catch Don Hutson out in the clear, seeing an end zone ahead. Smith's conversion wrapped the package up and tied a ribbon on it, 29–13, and afterward Frank Thomas sounded like the latter-day Bryant after a win when he said, "Stanford has the greatest football team we met all season. . . . The most we can say is we're thankful we could win."

In the air, in Howell's domain, was the difference between Thomas's Tide and Tiny Thornhill's Stanford. Alabama gained 123 yards on the ground, but 214 passing with ten completions in thirteen attempts. Stanford rushed for 196 but completed only five of twenty-three passes for 92 yards.

Thomas's reward was a new five-year contract, and he was back in Pasadena on January 1, 1938, a loser this time to California, 13–0. The Rose Bowl of 1945 finished it for people like Alabama, for the Big Ten agreement followed Frank Thomas's last visit. The coach, who soon would fall ill and turn the reins over to Red Drew in 1947, finished in the Rose just as he came. Alabama mangled Southern California 34–14, with Harry Gilmer leading the way, and that left the record altogether magnificent for the Crimson Tide in the Rose Bowl of once-upon-a-time.

4

Once Upon a Mountaintop

June 8, 1950

THEY PLAYED THE U.S. Open Golf Championship at Merion, outside Philadelphia, that year, which was 1950. Lee Mackey Jr. and his Tuscaloosa friend Harold Williams drove up from Birmingham where they had qualified. Mackey got the last of four places available in trials at the Country Club of Birmingham. He shot 149 for thirty-six holes, 75 and 74.

On the way east, the two young men stopped to play in a pro tournament at Fort Wayne, Indiana. Neither made the thirty-six-hole cut, and they drove on through the warmth of early June, arrived at Merion, arranged for quarters at a private home where they were given instructions in the use of the back stairs for coming and going, played a practice round, gawked like many another tourist there, and waited.

Mackey was then twenty-six years old. He had been a caddy at Roebuck, won a couple of city tournaments around home, went away to three years of being Private Mackey overseas in World War II, and came home to work summers for Sam Byrd, the ex-Yankee outfielder who was pro at Plum Hollow in Michigan. Now he gave lessons occasionally in Birmingham, wanted a club job, but couldn't find one.

This was the Lee Mackey who would stand for one golden instant on top of the world of golf, hero of the sports pages, having it all come true like a kid would dream it, maybe, carrying clubs around Roebuck in Birmingham, learning the game bit by bit, always playing on Monday mornings when caddies could play free.

Lee Mackey's approach to a place in history was just as routine as I relate it now, many years from June of 1950 when Ben Hogan, returning to golf after a near-fatal accident, Sam Snead, Cary Middlecoff, Jimmy Demaret, Lloyd Mangrum, Dutch Harrison, young Julius Boros, and Skip Alexander were the players who got the play in the press beforehand. Middlecoff was the defending champion.

Mackey was one of the number of unknowns who manage to get themselves into an Open, usually shoot themselves out of it quickly, and return home as unnoticed as when they came. U.S. Open headlines are not for the obscure, and nothing had happened beforehand to indicate that fate would treat the young man out of Birmingham any differently from the rest. When he went up the back stairs to bed in the palatial home near the golf course on Wednesday night, June 7, 1950, not many in that part of the world knew he was in it.

Nor did they when he showed up at the first tee at Merion's east course on Thursday morning. It was a little after ten when he shook the hands of Robert Roos Jr., an amateur from San Francisco, and a pro named Joe Novick from Rocky River, Ohio, the other members of his threesome. Undistinguished company for an undistinguished Alabamian. The early gallery had gone ahead with Middlecoff. Later travelers waited for Hogan, who would use a five iron for a cane as he forced his way about the course, and for Snead. Maybe Sam would win himself an Open.

When Mackey hooked his drive off No. 1 into the deep rough, no one saw it go except Mackey and Novick and Roos, three caddies who wouldn't have been happy about going to work with golfers not likely

A moment to remember: Lee Mackey, minutes after his record round in the U.S. Open. (Courtesy *Philadelphia Bulletin* and Temple University Archives)

to play past the second round, and a lady to keep score. The morning was hot, promising that the afternoon would be broiling. Not a cloud was in the sky. There was a bit of a breeze, enough to cool but not enough to affect a golf shot.

The rough was long at Merion, for it is demanded that Open courses be challenging, a fact of life that often disturbs latter-day professionals who see grass in the rough grown to six inches as completely unfair.

Mackey was in it. The round had begun exactly as it was supposed to begin for a twenty-six-year-old pro from Birmingham playing in his first Open. This was the pattern, built on long tradition.

Mackey's second shot was in the best manner of the unknowns, also. He came out of the rough with an iron and hooked the ball into a deep trap guarding the green. The par-four, 360-yard hole had him by the throat.

What no one knew or suspected was that this day, on this golf course, something special had been saved up for Lee Mackey Jr., whose father was playing at about the same time in an invitational tournament at the Selma Country Club. Now, the special something showed. Mackey's blast from the trap was within inches of the cup. He tapped it in for a par. Not bad for the crew-cut six-footer from Birmingham.

A par five waited for Mackey on the 595-yard second hole and a par three on the 195-yard third. Mackey worked them over quickly. He wouldn't dawdle on a shot. Sam Byrd had taught him to walk up and hit the thing. That's the way he played, saying little to anyone, concentrating fiercely because now he could feel a good day of golf rising in him. How good it would be, not even Lee Mackey could suspect at that point, as the threesome moved slowly. Middlecoff was slow, ahead, and Roos and Novick were scrambling.

Mackey's tee shot was not hit well on the fourth, and his second put him back in that awful rough, 130 yards from the green on a par-five, 561-yard hole. The pin was near the front of the green, and there was a small stream between Mackey and that green. His high pitch met the need perfectly. He was twelve feet past the hole, but his putt coming back was in for a birdie four. Now Mackey was one under par.

He was on in two, down for a par on the 425-yard fifth, with an eight-footer going in, and he parred again on the sixth, 435 yards. Grim-faced, feeling it, Mackey marched on. He was about to own this golf course. It was his baby.

Smartly, Mackey came off the tee with an iron on the seventh, a 350-yard par four that was prepared to penalize the wanderer. His first was out in the middle, his second was ten feet from the pin. His third was a putt that clunked home for another birdie. Eight was a birdie three also, with a twelve-footer hunting the cup like a homing pigeon.

On No. 9, a 185-yard par three, Mackey was forced to come from a trap, and he almost holed out. Par was a tap, and he had made the turn in 33, three under, but the posting of the score brought no gallery. The three golfers, the three caddies, and the lady scorekeeper went on in relative solitude.

The tenth hole was a par four, with Mackey's putt for a birdie no more than three inches short. That was an easy hole, comparatively speaking. The eleventh was a monster. It was here that Gene Sarazen had taken a seven in the 1934 Open, costing him the championship. The hole ran 367 yards downhill, and 275 yards away a creek crossed the fairway and came winding back in front of the green, on around behind it. Mackey's three wood from the tee was a refusal to gamble with the water. Then he pitched on, twenty feet from the cup. On days like that June day, twenty-foot putts fall. This one did, and that was another birdie. Mackey was four under par.

He got his par on No. 12 with a tough downhiller of about ten feet after his second shot had come off the green under the impetus of terrific backspin. They came to No. 13. For the first time, many people were watching, but chiefly because the green was close to the clubhouse. Maybe two thousand had ringed it. The hole was a par three of 133 yards. Mackey's tee shot was within two feet of the hole, and the fifth birdie was easy.

Now there was a gallery. Middlecoff was being deserted up ahead, and watchers were swarming from behind to see this golfer they'd never heard of who now was five under par, tearing a tough course apart. If they bothered Mackey, he gave no sign. The fourteenth was 425 yards. Mackey was on in two, straight as a string with everything he hit, but his twenty-foot putt for a birdie was uphill. He missed by inches getting it home.

On the 395-yard fifteenth, thinking not of a record but of holding what he had, Mackey came down the middle on his drive. Because the pin was on the right of the green, immediately behind a bunker, and because mean-looking rough was behind the green, Mackey played safe. He hit his iron to the middle of the green, and that left him a twenty-eight-foot putt. So what's twenty-eight feet? He sank it. The unknown from Birmingham was six under par with three holes to play.

Two just-right shots left Mackey a ten-foot putt for a birdie on the sixteenth. He barely missed, and took his par. On the 230-yard par-three seventeenth, which had a narrow green more than a hundred feet long, his first shot barely stayed on, at the very back. His first putt was five feet short. He missed the second, for par, by an inch, and he had his first bogey of the day.

The eighteenth was supposed to be Merion's most difficult hole. It was 458 yards across a canyon. Golf gallery estimates vary, but Roos, the amateur, wrote afterward that at least four thousand people were following Mackey at this point, and three thousand were around the green. Lee Mackey had never hit a golf shot before so many people in all his life.

Mackey's drive ticked the front part of the tee as it left, and barely cleared the abandoned rock quarry which made that vast hole in the fairway, but it had good roll and it was in the middle.

The thousands waited, whispering among themselves, as Mackey came up for his second shot. He took a three wood, and he hit it true, and when the ball stopped, with the crowd roaring its delight, Mackey was ten feet away from another birdie.

Here was a putt for a man to think about, to study, to worry over. Mackey walked up to it, looked, set himself, and knocked it in for the birdie three almost in less time than it takes to tell, and he had a 64 for the day. No one ever had shot a 64 in the U.S. Open. Lee Mackey Jr. of Birmingham, Alabama, had never shot a 64 anywhere, but there it was, and history had found him.

History liked him, too. The sportswriters and fans swarmed around him, because no one in half a century of U.S. Opens had done what the poker-faced twenty-six-year-old in the light beige slacks, plaid shirt, and blue suede shoes had done. "How, how, how?" they kept on asking him, and he praised Byrd for teaching him and he said, "I stayed out of the rough," and, "I kept trying to protect what I had and play it safe and the first thing I knew I had it, that's all."

The photographers grabbed him and they posed him kissing the golf ball and marking up his score and everything photographers can think of. Tomorrow, Friday, his face would be looking out from sports pages in every city in the land.

Obscure? Not Lee Mackey. To make the story better, some would write that he was penniless, almost hungry, and rags-to-riches. This wasn't the case. Lee Mackey Sr. was a well-to-do Birmingham businessman who had loaned his son the money for the trip.

But Lee Mackey Jr. was once-in-a-lifetime viewed from any angle, and they were agog on Thursday night all over Birmingham and Alabama at golf places, and what most people said was, "Who'd have thought it!" His dad made plans to fly up from Selma, and he'd never been on an airplane in his life, if Lee scored well on Friday. His telephone call home was sheer joy there. Harold Williams had had a 69, and wasn't that something, too?

Mackey and Williams were using the front steps when they went out the next day to be reminded that those whom fate embraces, fate can also cast aside. Mackey spent the second round of the 1960 U.S. Open in the rough. No putts would go in. He shot an 81, then had 75 and 77, finishing in a tie for twenty-first as Hogan won a playoff and took charge of golf again.

Mackey won a hundred dollars. He would try in a couple of other Opens, with indifferent success, before settling down to family and business and weekend golf in Birmingham, where he qualified for the trip to history, one magnificent moment on a mountain. He doesn't quarrel with himself over what happened next. The 64 cannot be taken away. It is forever.

5

The Rocket Eight

February 25, 1956

JOHN FRANCIS DEE JR. WAS twenty-nine years old when he came to Tuscaloosa to coach Alabama basketball in 1952. Four years later he left, driving a new automobile that had been given him by grateful alumni, back on the trail that eventually would return him to Notre Dame, and that's where he was headed all along. John Francis left a heap of history behind.

Dee had played at Notre Dame and had been an assistant coach there. He was a chunky five feet nine, cocky, Chicago-Irish and smart. He brought a basketball team with him to Alabama, five freshmen recruited carefully from midwestern country he had watched for Notre Dame. Dee was going in with aces wired, and they were George Linn from Columbus, Ohio; Dennis O'Shea from Toledo; Dick Gunder from Marion, Ohio; Leon Marlaire from Bradley, Illinois; and Jerry Harper, his big man, a gawky six-foot-eight freshman from Louisville. There were others, but these would be the heart of it—talented, bright, good-looking youngsters who knew what Dee meant when he told them, "From now on, you will be University of Alabama men.

Whatever you do, good or bad, you will be identified with this university. Make it good. Make them proud of you."

Dee marched before them, burning with excitement and with ambition, a new head coach with a million ideas and ready to challenge the world. He and his men would beat Kentucky and Adolph Rupp, he said, and they would win a Southeastern Conference championship for Alabama. They would make their game big. Listen to Dee and you might have gotten the impression that the game George Gipp really played at Notre Dame was basketball. Watch Dee work and you suspected that the man who must have taught him was Knute Rockne.

When Dee's men went out to play basketball, they went with fire in their eyes. He psyched them in the dressing room and psyched in the newspapers. His practices were lessons in change of pace, in war and peace. Dee stormed, Dee purred, and all the time he kept on selling his basketball players to themselves. "He made us think we were better than we were," Leon Marlaire told me once. "He could have sold bathing suits to Eskimos. I was going to Illinois to play basketball before he came to my house. My parents loved him by the time he had been in there five minutes. I don't suppose it took me much longer than that. What a guy!"

They were only so-so, playing as freshmen, but the fact that they could play as freshmen in the Southeastern Conference had been a factor in their recruiting. As sophomores they were better, and now the master plan, the Johnny Dee diagram for Alabama, was taking shape.

As juniors—growing still—they would lose their second straight game to Kentucky, at Lexington, and this was a Kentucky that won twenty-three and lost three on the way to one of Adolph Rupp's many Southeastern Conference championships. The score was 66–52, but the Tide team they called the "Rocket Eight" was acting like a contender, and the night they lost at Lexington was one they could laugh about when, in later years, they'd get together and talk, mostly about the fiery one who'd been their coach.

Kentucky was home and favored, and the immense Coliseum would be jammed to capacity to see the Wildcats do in Alabama, because this young Coach Dee kept on saying things for the papers about Rupp and Kentucky that Kentuckians regarded as downright irreverent. The morning of the game, Dee left his regulars wondering what he was up to and went off to huddle with substitutes who would not play in the game.

"Here's your chance, men," he told them. "You can shake them up. You can help this team more tonight than you ever have before." His subs, linked in conspiratorial partnership with their coach, waited only to be told which of the Kentucky players they should kidnap, or whatever it was Coach Dee wanted of them. What he wanted was quite simple.

"When we go out to warm up," he told them, "you will see those Kentucky guys walking up to half court, and they'll fold their arms across their chests and they'll be looking down their noses at us. I want you to walk right up there to the line and look 'em right in the eye, and I don't want you to take anything off of them, either. Nothing, you understand." They understood.

It happened just as Dee had forecast. Here came the Wildcats. There went the Tide, and it was a sight to be seen, a confrontation. Eye-to-eye, jowl-to-jowl, as a later Alabama football coach might have described it. They stood there for a long minute, or maybe it was two, and then there was a sudden flurry and basketball players were swinging it out in the middle of the court as state troopers, planning only to enjoy a game, found themselves forced to duty. There was an immense pileup, and Jim Bogan, a center from Chicago, was bitten in the chest. He said later he thought Happy Chandler's boy did it, though he wasn't sure, but he was proud of his battle scar.

The officers brought an armistice quickly, and now the boos fell down from the top of the Coliseum and rolled across anything from Alabama that moved. The troopers stood guard behind the Alabama bench as play commenced. For a good while, Dee's shake-'em-up tactics looked like they might work. It was late in the game before Kentucky got loose for good. Dee never would plead guilty to the charge that the excitement was prearranged, but the players saw him grinning after defeat, and that never had been seen before. Then their fighting comrades let them in on the secret.

"He was always pulling something," remembers Linn, who became captain as a senior, and the Rocket Eight remembered a night against Georgia Tech in Atlanta in their last year, the great year, as one of Dee's neatest, Dee at his Rockne-like best.

Alabama had lost a game to Notre Dame in the Sugar Bowl tournament, had lost to North Carolina and St. John's on a swing through the East, but now was moving along, winning them all in the conference race, and Alabama was supposed to be winning at Georgia Tech. At the half Georgia Tech led.

The players were in the dressing room, seated, looking up at the blank blackboard where Dee would diagram defenses and plays when the coach came from the outside, and they were certain they'd never seen such an angry man in all their young lives.

"Well, girls," he said, and his sarcasm flayed them.

He walked to the blackboard and picked up a piece of chalk, threw it to the floor, looked at his players, drew back his right arm, and rammed his fist through the board. Next they heard his voice from the shower room, out of sight but not nearly out of range: "I have never been so embarrassed in my life. I'm not going back out there. You can go if you want to. I may catch a plane to Tuscaloosa. I can't stand watching you any more."

Then, silence.

Finally, the players filed out, leaving their coach behind, and it was time to start the second half. "Will he come out?" Marlaire whispered anxiously to Linn, the captain. "Sure he will," said Linn, but the officials were walking toward the Alabama team, and Dee was nowhere to be seen.

The game began again, and Alabama's Rocket Eight got itself together. Somehow, this seemed important. They had gone past ten minutes in the second half, had caught up, had gone ahead when Dee eased himself back onto the bench and signaled for Linn to call a time-out. The captain did, and the players came for what instructions the coach might have now. They gathered around. "Now, you're my *boys*," he told them, and smiled a saintly smile, and Alabama went on and finished up the assignment.

They used up January, winningly, and headed into February the same way. The race was close in the SEC. There was no place for slowing down, nothing permitted except win, win, win as the pressure grew and the climax of all that Dee and the five, plus Jim Fulmer of Florence, Jack Kubiszyn of Buffalo, and Dale Shuman of Savannah, struggled to attain. The starters and the three reserves added up to eight for "Rocket Eight," and it was Dee himself who gave the group the name that stuck.

February 25, 1956, at Montgomery in the Coliseum—and would you believe it, people were scalping basketball tickets!—was when every dream came true. It was Saturday, and more than ten thousand had jammed themselves into that place to see Alabama battle Kentucky. Three games remained after the Wildcats, but here was the giant hurdle that had to be cleared. Time and circumstance rendered this Alabama basketball's most magnificent hour, the biggest game Alabama ever played and won.

Alabama started on top but couldn't shake away from an iron-fisted Kentucky defense. After twelve minutes the Tide was leading by seven points, 25–18, as Marlaire, one of the smallest men on the floor, came flying through the air to tip in a rebound. The pace was vigorous, also slow.

With five minutes left in the first half, Alabama led 31–24, but a hot streak by Bob Burrow, the big Kentucky center, moved the Wildcats quickly into striking distance. Burrow scored twelve straight points over a four-minute span, and the twelfth one put Kentucky ahead 36–35. Gunder hit, and Alabama had its lead back and kept it. The score was 43–40 at intermission. It looked close, but actually it wasn't. This game was about to be real, real easy.

Three minutes after the teams came back into the din and the

On the way to 101 against Kentucky: Dick Gunder dunks two points.
(Courtesy *Tuscaloosa News*)

glare of the overflowing arena, Alabama still held on, but only by a point at 51–50. Then that Coliseum exploded. You had to see it to believe it. Linn started it with a jumper, came back for two free throws, and socked in another free throw. This had taken a minute. Marlaire scored from far out, and away they went. With nine minutes to play Alabama was a 78–52 leader. What that amounted to was twenty-seven points in seven minutes for the Rocket Eight and only two for the Wildcats, those on free throws.

It was all over as far as the winning and losing were concerned, but this cake needed icing. That came only seventeen seconds from the finish. It was 99–76, Kentucky with the ball and trying to hold on to it, when Linn stole a pass, flipped the ball out ahead of him, picked it up for a dribble, and went driving for a layup. He twisted, spun the ball away, and it swished through quick and easy-like, and then the game was over. Alabama had won 101–77.

For the first time in all of the wonderful basketball history of Rupp's Wildcats, an opponent had gone over 100 points against them. This, then, was the highest total ever recorded against Kentucky, perennial champion of the Southeast. City College of New York had scored 89 on a Rupp team in 1950. The record was a wreck.

"I don't remember ever being keyed up for such a ball game," Marlaire says now. "I remember at the half Johnny told us, 'It's your ball game if you want it,' and I remember something else, too, which isn't as bad as it might sound. Johnny told us, 'The first time there is a jump ball in the second half, or a rebound, I want every Alabama man going as tough as he can go. That's all right if there are five fouls. They can call only one. We're going to show them who's boss.'"

Who was boss was Alabama. Harper, the Kentuckian who got away, led scoring with thirty-seven points, and the six-foot-eight center owned the backboards. He snatched away twenty-six rebounds. Linn scored twenty-seven, Gunder nineteen, Marlaire thirteen, and Dee had his new car to drive home from victory on Sunday morning. Jimmy Marlowe of Tuscaloosa had made the presentation to him twenty minutes before the game started.

The Rocket Eight went on to beat Tennessee, then Auburn, and locked up the championship against Florida at Gainesville on March 5. Having played as freshmen, the five seniors couldn't go to the NCAA tournament. Dee took them instead to the national AAU tournament, entered as Ada Oil, sponsored by Texan Bud Adams. They lost to Phillips 66 on a last-second shot in the final. This was big, but it was nothing to compare with the Saturday night in Montgomery when Alabama did all that Johnny Dee had said they would do.

Later that March, the itchy-footed Mr. Dee resigned and coached for a while in the AAU league, took a turn with the pros, went into law practice at Denver, and at last in 1964 was named head coach at Notre Dame. Harper, Marlaire, and Linn married Alabama girls and became Alabamians for good. Kubiszyn stayed, too, to star after the Rocket Eight had finished its tour, which put Alabama basketball on a peak it had never known before or since.

Marlaire, working for a trucking firm in Birmingham, was out with a friend one night in the summer of 1967, and the friend was proud to introduce him to someone else. "He was on the Rocket Eight, you know," was how it went. "Oh," the man said, "you in the automobile business?" Marlaire grinned, said no, and remembered how it was on February 25, 1956, at Montgomery.

6

Third Down, Glory to Go

September 28, 1957

LLOYD NIX OF KANSAS, ALABAMA, looked at the faces of the ten young men around him. They looked right back and waited, and twenty-year-old Nix, playing his first college game at quarterback, was alone, though forty-two thousand people shivering under raincoats and umbrellas in Shields-Watkins Field at Knoxville and eleven Tennessee Volunteers waited, too, to see what he would do.

Nix had hunted up the first-down marker as he walked to the huddle, out in the rain and the cold of September 28, 1957, in Auburn's first game of the season, which would move from this beginning to the brightest hours War Eagle football had ever known. This was the beginning of a national championship, though not even Ralph Jordan the coach or Nix the quarterback—or anyone else for that matter—could have dreamed even of such when they flew into Knoxville the day before.

Third down, six yards away from a first down, and underdog Auburn was being slowed again by a Tennessee defense that already had stopped these upstarts at the one and at the eight. You run out of chances eventually, break the back of an offense by going again and again and again and yet again and stopping short.

Nix said, "Thirty-seven, H, Belly," and if the other faces were surprised, they didn't show it. Their owners clapped their hands together, sloshed through the muck back to the line of scrimmage, and for all any man can say, Auburn might have won the football championship of the collegiate United States at that instant.

Thirty-seven, H, Belly was the old belly play made famous first by Eddie LeBaron at College of the Pacific. The quarterback took the ball, shoved it into his fullback's stomach, but kept his hands on it as the fullback moved toward the line. He might keep it, the quarterback might take it back, then might run himself, or might pitch out to a halfback trailing the play. There are three options.

But Thirty-seven, H, Belly had been dropped from the Auburn arsenal. It wasn't a Tiger play for Tennessee. This one was in the ashcan, discarded, but Lloyd Nix of Kansas, Alabama, who became a prosperous dentist in Decatur, Alabama, didn't have the kind of a brain that discarded things. He reached into his mind and found the answer for the moment.

Jackie Burkett, the sophomore center, slammed the ball into his quarterback's hands, and Nix moved to the right toward Billy Atkins, the fullback. The lines had met, fighting at each other across the mud, as Nix and Atkins moved together. Now Atkins went ahead, without the football. Nix had it, sliding between Tennessee's left end and left tackle. He was looking for Lamar Rawson, the right halfback, as he cleared the line of scrimmage and the Tennessee linebacker crashed into him. Somehow, Nix got rid of the football, and it was "a ground-skinner pitchout," he could laugh, telling about the play when his college years were done.

The grounder was straight to Rawson, however, for the Nix-Atkins maneuver had left him clear. The sophomore from Pensacola, first of the three brothers recruited for Auburn by defense coach Hal Herring, swept up the ball and drove at the goal. When Tennessee got Rawson stopped, Auburn had first down on the four. Three downs

Billy Atkins, who scored the game's only touchdown, breaks loose for nineteen yards. (Courtesy Auburn University)

later, Billy Atkins went into the end zone from the one, then stepped back and kicked the seventh point, and Auburn had won the first of ten games, 7–0.

The game's the thing, and though the record might show more dramatic scores than one touchdown to zero, the setting, the ultimate results of that season, and the fantastic career of Nix give the happenings of that miserably wet and wintry day in Knoxville high rank in the football history of Auburn and the South and the nation.

It hadn't been in the plan, either, that Nix would be at quarterback to direct the victory over Tennessee and nine others. At Carbon Hill High School he'd been a left-handed quarterback, good enough to be offered scholarships by twelve Southeastern Conference schools and a great many others, but in August before he'd enroll at Auburn, Nix found himself switched to halfback for the annual state high school all-star game at Tuscaloosa.

Another boy bound for Auburn, Charlie Bolton from Athens, would be the quarterback in the all-star game. Nix, an outstanding athlete who also excelled at baseball and basketball in high school, didn't let the switch bother him. He played an outstanding game at halfback. Afterward, Auburn coaches who'd seen it said, "We might just put you there when you get to school," and they did because the quarterback crop looked solid enough without Nix, who wasn't nearly as flashy-looking a fellow as some already on hand.

By the third game of his sophomore season, Lloyd Nix was a starting right halfback, and that was fine by him. Then he hurt a knee and missed several games, but he finished the season there and was a halfback still when spring practice for 1957 came on at Auburn. In September, a veteran quarterback had been dismissed from the squad. Help was needed. Ralph Jordan, the head coach who had come to Auburn in 1951 and made his alma mater's football bigger than it ever had been, checked the available, then told Nix, "You're it."

From September 1 to September 27, the Friday when Jordan and his squad flew into Knoxville to start the season, Nix had become entirely "it." He would be the starting quarterback for Jerry Wilson, Red Phillips, Zeke Smith, Tommy Lorino, Billy Atkins, Bobby Hoppe, Tim Baker, Dan Presley, and the rest of that most manly crew starting out on something big.

The year before, in Birmingham, as Auburn and Tennessee met again for the first time since 1939, the Tigers had met humiliation. All-American Johnny Majors had one of his greatest days in leading the orange-shirted Volunteers to a 35–7 runaway, and that put Tennessee on the road to the Sugar Bowl.

Leading off 1957 at home, the Vols were once again favored against an Auburn team with a quarterback who had never played the position and with too many sophomores expected to play. No one knew then that both Burkett and Smith would become all-Americans. Phillips, the end from Alexander City, already was well on the way, but there were simply too many Auburn question marks. Plus, Tennessee was at home, and Tennessee never has done much losing at old Shields-Watkins. Ask any man who's been there.

I was there that day, and I recall standing in the rain, waiting for the bus that would take the players and one sportswriter out early to where the action waited. George Atkins, a young assistant coach who had been an outstanding Auburn lineman and then a pro, stood with me and said, "Nobody knows how hard these boys have worked, and not too many people know how bad they want to win this game. There's no doubt at all in my mind. They're going to win it."

The Tigers played like that from the first kickoff, which Lorino took back eighteen yards to Auburn's thirty-seven. Nix knew what to do. He sent Hoppe and Lorino and Atkins to work inside the tackles. Atkins had an eleven-yard run, Hoppe a ten-yarder, Atkins a thirteen-yarder as they drove right off to first down on Tennessee's eight. From here, Nix made three, Atkins one, and a pass missed. On fourth down, Lorino was stopped on the one yard line and the Vols had rescued themselves.

Tennessee kicked out. Lorino ran the ball back twenty-three yards to the twenty-two, and the second team, quarterbacked by John Kern, got down to the eight before Atkins was called on for a fourth-down field goal try, which was wide.

A sixty-one-yard Tennessee quick kick set the Tigers back. Nix thought to return the favor, but Atkins's quick kick was blocked out of bounds on the Auburn eighteen. Suddenly, the picture had changed. Then it changed right back when Phillips leaped on a Tennessee fumble, and Lorino punted out. When the scoreless first quarter ended, Auburn had handled the ball on twenty-five plays, Tennessee for five.

They went into the second quarter, and the rain kept coming steadily. Never very hard, but incessant and icy, and it was a hard, tough football game, with some watchers beginning to think about a scoreless tie when Wilson broke in to get his hands on an Al Carter punt. The ball traveled six yards. Auburn went from its own forty-three toward the only touchdown it was going to need.

Hoppe and Atkins made a first down on Tennessee's forty-five. Lorino moved ahead three and Hoppe two, and Nix showed what he was made of with a third-down pass which he got to Wilson for ten yards with three Tennesseans bearing down on him. Now Auburn was on the thirty. It was Rawson for five, Atkins four, Rawson for seven. First down on the fourteen, and six thousand Auburn rooters in the dripping-wet crowd knew that this time they had to get there.

Lorino dived for three up the middle, then Atkins was stopped after a one-yard gain, and this is where we came in, for this is where Nix—cool and confident—put in the play he needed, and in a bit the Auburn people could be happy over developments, though they wouldn't sit easy until the end.

Auburn was still in charge of the murky battleground in the third quarter, getting to the Tennessee twenty-six before losing the ball on downs, to the nineteen where a field goal attempt was blocked. Late in the quarter Tennessee finally got a shot after a short Auburn punt, and the Vols got to the seventeen before Phillips and Wilson, successively, broke in to throw Tennessee runners for four-yard losses. Auburn took over at the twenty-five.

Late, late Bowden Wyatt's team marched from its thirty-four to a first down on the Auburn twenty-nine, driving the football, racing the clock. Wilson and Phillips went to work again, and Zeke Smith with them. On fourth down from the thirty-three, Al Carter the tailback went back for one last, desperate try. Phillips was after him, hounding him. Carter had retreated to the forty-seven when Big Red threw him down, and it was all over but the celebration, which was considerable. If you've ever seen Auburn loyalists celebrate an upset in football, you'll know what I mean. If you are one, you'll know even better.

There was time for Lloyd Nix to take two snaps into center, then War Eagles were counting down the last seconds. Suddenly it was over, and the boys out there were leaping for joy. For sheer jubilation, this moment might have eclipsed any I've ever seen in a lifetime of watching the playing of games.

This is what the *Birmingham News* had to say the next morning:

"The day was wet, dripping.

"It was cold and clammy and uncomfortable.

"A miserable sort of a September Saturday in Tennessee.

"The clouds hung low over the perilous battleground which was Shields-Watkins Field.

"Gray day, somber day, unhappy day for Tennesseans.

"For Auburn, it came out something altogether different.

"The sun was shining and birds must have been singing and all of that. Great day, wonderful day, happy for the team which came an underdog and stayed to conquer."

As evidenced, there was some joy in the press box too, and this was only a sample of what was to come. Auburn beat Chattanooga, Kentucky, Georgia Tech, Houston, Florida, Mississippi State, Georgia, and Florida State and wrapped up its No. 1 in the nation by walloping Alabama 40–0.

This was a team that, most of the time, seemed content to get done only what it had to do offensively, supremely confident that the defense could take care of the rest. Chattanooga scored a touchdown against Auburn in the 40–7 defeat. Houston got one while falling 48–7, and Mississippi State one in a 15–7 loss, the only game of the year in which the Tigers were called upon to come from behind. Florida State got the last of four touchdowns Auburn yielded while losing 29–7.

The Tigers went wheeling through 1958 undefeated again, though they were tied by Georgia Tech 7–7 and were making history as they went, led by a little quarterback from little Kansas, Alabama, who practically never made a mistake, who didn't run very fast or throw pretty passes left-handed, but who always got where he needed to go.

7

What Comebacks Are Made Of

November 12, 1960

IN THE FIRST HALF OF THEIR Grant Field game, Georgia Tech had made fifteen points and Alabama had made one first down and no points. So, this one shaped up as a routine 30–0 coaster for Tech.

If the football game had been close, Paul Bryant knew what he'd be doing at the half when Alabama's Crimson Tide came in to rest and check the strategy.

Bryant has a plan . . . for everything. Included are the specific words he'll use for specific situations, and it's part of the reason for his outstanding success in the world of college football, which will remember him forever like Rockne, like Warner, like Neyland.

So if Georgia Tech had put only that first touchdown by Jimmy Nail of Birmingham on the scoreboard in the first half of the game they played on sunny November 12, 1960, at Grant Field in Atlanta, the fierce Bryant would have been moving among his players. He wouldn't have interrupted the quick lecture from the assistant coach at the blackboard, but he would have gone to an individual here, another there, and his big hands would have clutched the boy's red jersey as he pulled him close and looked him dead in the eye.

"When are you going to start playing like Alabama?" he might have gritted at the football players, or, "Are you ready to quit letting those guys push you around?"

The technique would have been effective, 99 times out of 100, for as the all-American linebacker Lee Roy Jordan said once after he'd gone to be an outstanding pro with the Dallas Cowboys, "Coach Bryant *always* does the right thing."

But as the lights flicked off the last seconds of the second quarter on this Saturday at Grant Field, it wasn't a close football game at all. Georgia Tech was running away, and gave no sign of slowing down. Tech had scored a first-quarter touchdown, then added a forty-seven-yard field goal by Tommy Wells, and then Stan Gann tacked on a touchdown late in the second quarter for a 15–0 lead. Alabama had one first down.

Now, there would be a respite from misery. Alabama's players ran for their dressing room, and as Bryant loped down the sidelines across the field from the press box, in front of the jeering Tech student body, field-glass users checking his every move saw surely the calmest man in the house.

Now Alabama was inside, and the coaches spotting from the press box had come down to tell what they'd seen. This had been done well, that hadn't. Tech was doing this, was likely now to do that, and then the players seated on benches, half-sprawled on the floor, waited and watched as their head coach prepared to say his say. They wondered, too, what was coming, and half in dread because they knew it could be angry. It wasn't.

"You have played well enough to be ahead," Bryant said. "You would be ahead except for the mistakes. You will win if you go out there and do what you are supposed to do, like you are supposed to do it, and I believe you will do it. Now, let's go!"

The last words were a fire blazing, but no one had panicked, and no one was going to, and thus was set in motion what might have been the most remarkable comeback ever put together by a Bryant-coached Alabama football team, for when the football game was over,

Alabama had won 16–15. At the half, all of Georgia Tech knew that this pesky new nemesis surely would be beaten 30–0. Loyal Tech men still have difficulty believing that what took place really ever happened. It was impossible. But it wasn't.

Too many things had to fall in place. Here was a jigsaw puzzle that couldn't be worked, but Alabama found a football hero for every need—a hand, a foot, a heart—and Alabama won.

Georgia Tech must have sensed a difference as soon as the third quarter was kicked off. This wasn't the same team the Engineers had mauled the first thirty minutes, having their happy way. This was something else.

Twice, Tech had the football. Twice, Tech was stopped. Then a fourteen-yard punt by Gerald Burch opened the door.

Mike Fracchia fair-caught the shortie that had almost been blocked, and Alabama was on the Tech forty-nine. For the first time, Pat Trammell, the coach-on-the-field quarterback from Scottsboro, had room to operate. Operate, he and his friends did.

Fracchia ran, Trammell ran, and he hit an eighteen-yard pass to Leon Fuller. Finally, Alabama was on the three and little Fuller drove it over the goal in two tries. A pass for a two-point conversion was botched, but Alabama clearly was on the way to something. Now it was a football game, 15–6, which was the way the fourth quarter began with Trammell hurt and out. Bob Skelton from Pell City came to be the quarterback, nine points behind, the Georgia Tech end zone eighty-seven yards away.

Skelton's Tide career had been somewhat checkered. Once, in Bryant's tough, early days of reshaping Alabama football, he had quit the squad, but the little battler had come back. If he hadn't, that magnificent November 12 might never have been. That was one piece that had fallen into place.

First down from the thirteen, and Skelton promptly dispatched the power-running Fracchia up the middle for twenty-two yards to the thirty-five. Butch Wilson lost three yards, then Fracchia was stopped, so Skelton took charge himself. He ran right end for twelve to the forty-four, and the fourth-and-one gamble with Fracchia made four to a first down on the forty-eight.

One pass missed, but the next one went to Skelton's Pell City buddy, Jerry Spruiell, all the way to Tech's twenty-four. Fracchia hammered out four, then Skelton went sprinting, spinning, refusing to go down until he had reached the eight yard line. Bingo, touchdown! On first down from the eight, Skelton pitched to Norbie Ronsonet in the end zone.

Tommy Brooker, Alabama's placekicker, was injured. Richard O'Dell, who had never kicked in a game, came on to try the extra point and made it. Georgia Tech's lead had been cut to 15–13 with 8:44 to play. There was time enough—just barely, but enough.

Gambling all the way, the Tide lost the ball on downs by inches on its forty with 5:17 showing on the clock. This was supposed to mean that school was out, but the defense Jordan led forced a punt and Alabama set out again from its twenty. There were three minutes, twenty-one seconds for covering eighty yards. Could Skelton? Skelton could.

Bob passed to Tommy White for first down on the thirty, hit Fuller for nine, and Fuller made the first down by inches on the forty. Skelton to Bill Battle was a first down on Tech's forty-two. Alabama called time-out with a minute and thirty-four seconds of agony to go.

Skelton to Billy Piper was incomplete. Skelton to Battle was long. Burch broke in to throw Skelton for a three-yard loss back at the forty-five. Fourth down and thirteen. Stop this one, and the show was over, but Skelton found Ronsonet open on the Tech thirty-two and put the football there for another first down. The clock was going, going, going . . .

Skelton went back once more, came up almost to the line, stepping between frantic tacklers, and threw once more. The crowd was counting seconds after Butch Wilson caught it on the six. Alabama scrambled to line up after the referee finally got away from the football. Some said Skelton shoved him away, but Skelton says he didn't.

Somehow, the kicking tee got there. Somehow, Skelton knelt and

Bobby Skelton (11) was a prime mover in the Tide's great comeback against Georgia Tech. (Courtesy *Tuscaloosa News*)

called for the ball, and the thousands were on their feet, screaming. It was a moment gone quite insane. Then the ball was back, and Skelton got it down and twenty-year-old Richard O'Dell from Lincoln, Alabama, stepped once, twice, and swung his right foot into this football. It was on its way.

There have been, in the history of the game of football, placekicks that were much prettier than that one. The ball was jerked up, high, fluttering, sort of, then it was a wounded pigeon, dying as it fell toward the goalposts. Did it? Didn't it?

The game was over. The clock had run out of time when Referee Johnny Lynch threw his hands high over his head to signal, it did. The first and only field goal Richard O'Dell would ever kick at in his entire football career was gone, and Alabama had won 16–15. The final piece was in place.

There had been many others. For instance, if Billy Richardson hadn't blocked the extra point after Georgia Tech's first touchdown, and if Wells hadn't missed a second, O'Dell would never have been kicking at a field goal to win the game. If Skelton hadn't been there . . . if Lee Roy Jordan, sophomore linebacker, hadn't played like an all-American long before he would become one . . . if, if, and if, and Tech could find a hundred places where the game could have been won. It's always that way when defeat comes narrowly.

This was a third straight for the new Alabama, Bryant's Alabama, over Georgia Tech, and the Crimson Tide would go on to take six out of seven before Tech broke off the series because, as Dr. Edwin Harrison, the president, told Alabama's Dr. Frank Rose, "We like to go to bowls. This is too hard a game for us in November."

It was, for a fact, very hard. It made bitter pills for swallowing, but never more so than on November 12, 1960, when it could be written like this for the *Birmingham News* the next morning:

"The score was 16–15.

"Numbers in lights on a scoreboard.

"Flip a switch. They're gone.

"But Alabama's Crimson Tide put them there Saturday at Grant Field and left them flaming for history.

"Wildly, magnificently, unbelievably, impossibly, Alabama came storming back from deep despair on this beautiful Autumn afternoon and left Georgia Tech stunned . . . and beaten. . . .

"For 30 minutes, this was Georgia Tech's field. Tech led, 6–0, 9–0, 15–0, and Alabama fought for its life.

"For 59 minutes, 59 seconds, this was Georgia Tech's football game.

"Then all of a sudden, all of it was gone. . . .

"Hutson . . . Howell . . . Hubert . . . Sington . . . Campbell . . . Suther . . . Gilmer . . . Kilgrow . . . Rose Bowl . . . Sugar . . . Cotton and Orange. This team on this Saturday matched them all and left a treasure for the memories of all Tide men.

"They were beaten, but they wouldn't be. They were run out of Grant Field but they came back.

"If the words are extravagant, so were they."

And the big man with the strong, calm face had stood before them in the dressing room, his team one step away from disaster, and he told them: "You can win."

It is obvious that Trammell, Skelton, Fracchia, Wilson, Piper, Ronsonet, Fuller, O'Dell, and all of them believed him down to the twenty-four-yard field goal which made that Saturday night one of the happiest Saturday nights University of Alabama people ever spent in the city of Atlanta, Georgia, after a football game.

8

Improbable Hero

January 1, 1964

THE SUGAR BOWL DIDN'T LOOK LIKE the Sugar Bowl when Paul Bryant took Alabama's football team out there on December 31, 1963, for a look at the place where the Crimson Tide would start the new year the next day against Mississippi.

The name was the same, and the location, but maybe they'd have to rename this one the Snow Bowl. Airborne white stuff coming in for a landing on New Orleans covered everything, and still it kept coming. The people would throw snowballs at one another in something new for New Year's Eve celebrations down along Bourbon Street that night.

Dr. Tim Davis, who then was Tim Davis, University of Alabama senior, remembers that someone had built a snowman out front of the stadium, and a photographer came to Coach Bryant beneath the stands asking for players to pose with the snowman in a picture for the morning paper.

Bryant made it funny. He laughed with his football players, too. He pointed to Grady Elmore and then beckoned to Davis. "I want you two," Bryant said. "We can't have somebody who's going to do much playing going out in that cold and catching flu."

So Tim Davis's picture was made in the snow. The photographer who got it would regard himself as extremely fortunate along about sundown the next day. He might even wonder if all that business about Bryant being psychic wasn't true after underdog Alabama had jumped on Ole Miss and written a memorable chapter for Crimson Tide history.

This was because Tim Davis of Columbus, Georgia, spent the afternoon of January 1, 1964, in New Orleans kicking field goals through uprights, over crossbars, into snowbanks beyond, built when the tarpaulin covering the field was cleared. Davis kicked four of them in a record-wrecking performance, and he missed a fifth from fifty yards, just by a little, and Alabama won 12–7.

It wasn't all Tim Davis, not by a mile. There was a sophomore quarterback from Cleveland, Tennessee, named Steve Sloan, who had taken over for the suspended Joe Namath. Sloan was a nineteen-year-old kid thrown into a pressure cooker, and if the assignment bothered him at all, it never showed for an instant.

Eddie Versprille was there, and Steve Allen, Benny Nelson, Paul Crane, Gaylon McCollough, Gary Martin, Billy Piper, Butch Henry, Jack Hurlbut, Steve Wright, Jimmy Dill, Mickey Andrews, Mike Fracchia, Al Lewis, and Bill Wieseman, and they and their friends were outweighed twenty pounds to the man by the undefeated Southeastern Conference champions from Mississippi, but it never seemed to matter at all.

They held Ole Miss to 77 yards on the ground, gave up 171 in the air, but knocked down nine passes and intercepted one, and, most important of all, jumped on six of the eleven fumbles that fell from Rebel fingers. These Tidesmen moved the football to fourteen first downs, 165 rushing yards with Sloan getting 51 of it on sixteen tries, but the points they had to have all came from one thin, studious-looking youngster who could do nothing except kick. That was his job. And that left him the big, big story of this football game.

You go back to a high school football field at Tifton, Georgia, in 1957 to find out what made the Sugar Bowl of 1964 come out the way it did. There you find the shaping of one of the unlikeliest heroes of one of the most wildly improbable postseason football games ever played anywhere.

In 1957, Alvin Davis, who had played at Alabama, where they knew him as "Pig" Davis, and then turned to coaching, had a son coming into his sophomore year of high school football. He was a quarterback, and a good one. A little on the light side, but he'd put on weight, and he could throw the ball well. He could think even better, and if called upon to do so he could kick the thing out of sight.

So the future was laid out for Pig Davis's eldest, Tim. He'd finish high school, and then he'd be a college quarterback, and who knew what richness of life lay beyond? It was a good dream built of solid substance.

Like many another dream that has been dreamed since the beginning of time, this one didn't come true, because Tim Davis's sophomore season was brought up short by an injury to his right knee. An operation followed. The boy would not put on a football suit again in high school. As a junior, as a senior, he watched from the stands, and he must have longed for what might have been.

But the doctors had said "That's all," so that was all for the boy who had been a quarterback.

Now, there are several ways to handle a dream that's gone bust, and some of them aren't good, but if you're Tim Davis you hunt up a substitute. If you're Tim Davis, who can't play quarterback anymore, you find another road. Tim's road was day after day of placekicking, out on his own, strengthening the leg and the knee that had let him down, adding distance, improving accuracy, working at it.

College coaches out looking for high school talent to become college talent saw Pig Davis's boy kick, and the reports went back to Tuscaloosa, Atlanta, Auburn—all over. Then came the scholarship offers. Tim Davis weighed them and finally boiled it down to Georgia Tech and Alabama.

When at last he was face-to-face with the man whose school he'd chosen, he looked the coach square in the eye and gave him his terms.

"I don't want to come to Alabama if you're just doing this out of friendship," the youngster told Paul Bryant, and he got stern, quick reassurance. Bryant wasn't handing out Alabama scholarships to anyone, then or now, because of friendship. He was building, then. He was getting things back like they were in the long ago of Wallace Wade and after him Frank Thomas.

"We want you because you can help us," Bryant said, "and we can help you," and Davis signed his grant-in-aid happily.

The specialist from Tifton, Georgia (later Columbus, where the family moved), came to Tuscaloosa kicking. In his first freshman game, his first football game since he had been a sophomore in high school, Davis kicked three extra points. He missed a couple, he thinks, because he had grown unaccustomed to the sound of the turmoil about him, but he knew this would pass, and it did.

In 1961 he lettered and kicked for a national championship team as a sophomore. He was busy on duty again in 1962, and in 1963. He hit many of them, big for Alabama, extra points and field goals, but the first day of 1964, the last day he would stick his shoe in a football, is the one that won't let itself be forgotten.

The 1963 season hadn't been the kind that Bryant-spoiled Alabama fans now were demanding of their team. The Tide lost to Florida 10–6 and to Auburn 10–8, and then, a week after the Auburn loss, with a late-televised game with Miami coming up and the Sugar Bowl already announced, Namath, the star quarterback, was dropped from the squad for violating training rules. Another year and he would redeem himself fully and sign a fabulous pro contract with the New York Jets.

But it was a team without a quarterback that went into Mobile the week before the Sugar Bowl for final preparation, a team that Mississippi certainly would handle on January 1 in New Orleans. The underdogs were getting grim about it before they took the bus down to the coast to the bowl town two days before the show. They would have a new quarterback, Sloan. Also a placekicker who now wasn't kicking at all.

Davis had gone, at this juncture, to Carney Laslie, the assistant who works with kickers, and told him, "I'd like not to kick anymore before the game, coach," and Laslie had granted the rather strange request after conferring with Bryant. The youngster explained, "It's like a pitcher's arm," referring to his leg. He was leg-weary. He worried about going stale.

Then there was the snow, which stopped transportation into New Orleans and left many a Tide and Rebel fan home preparing to watch on television as the teams moved out in the early afternoon's chill, the field cleared and dry, the kickoff drawing close.

Davis would kick about fourteen times, warming up. He drove a couple down the field, then turned to Laslie beside him, grinning, feeling good.

"Coach," Tim said, "if we need a long one, I think I can do it today."

He was to have the opportunity.

Alabama had defensive answers, and Alabama had offense with its new quarterback for a seventy-two-yard first-quarter drive that went to the Mississippi twenty-one. On fourth and one Bryant sent his kicker to work.

They huddled. Benny Nelson set himself exactly six and two-thirds yards back of the line, which is where Bryant wants his holder, and practice makes the position automatic. McCollough snapped. Nelson got the ball down. Then it was away, dead on target, high enough, long enough, over the bar, between the uprights into the snow. Alabama led 3–0.

In the second quarter, Butch Henry got one of those fumbles on the Rebel thirty-one. The aroused Mississippians weren't yielding easily. On fourth from the thirty-six Tim Davis was out again for one step, two step, kick, and that made it 6–0. It would become 9–0 on a twenty-two-yarder ten seconds before halftime after the Tide had gotten to the five and couldn't go in. Statistics told a story in addition to the score. At intermission, Ole Miss had been held to seventeen yards rushing, fifteen passing.

Close by a snowbank in the Sugar Bowl, Tim Davis hits one of his four field goals. (Courtesy *Birmingham News*)

In the third quarter, Davis took a shot at a fifty-yarder, and it was long enough but wide. Then, after Billy Piper intercepted a pass on Alabama's forty-one and Fracchia, Sloan, and Andrews got the ball to the Rebel thirty-two, Tim slugged a finale, forty-eight yards. This was more points than Alabama would need, though down in the final, nerve-rending minutes no one could have been sure. No one was, until it was over.

Ole Miss came alive, finally, for a seventy-four-yard drive that was capped by a Perry Lee Dunn pass to Larry Smith for a touchdown. Billy Carl Irwin kicked the Rebels' seventh point, and the Mississippians in the crowd of 80,873 took new hope. Now this frustration surely would end.

When Sloan fumbled to the Rebs on Alabama's thirty-two after the kickoff, that's exactly how it looked. Dunn shot a twenty-three-yard pass to Fred Roberts to the nine, then charged through for six to the three. It was second down. Here it was, the moment of truth, and here was the time and the place for Bryant's Crimson Tidesmen to reach deep for the extra. They did. They found it.

Second and three. Dunn was stopped for a one-yard loss by Wieseman. Third and four now. Dunn threw to Allen Brown deep in the end zone, too deep. Brown fell into the snowbank back there, beyond the last line, juggling the ball. Fourth and four, and Dunn rolled left. The 202-pound Rebel quarterback was turning the corner toward the goal when Wieseman, Hurlbut, and Versprille met him, and that was the end of the line.

Alabama kicked out. Mississippi came back, and there still was time. From the Tide forty-one, Dunn passed to Mike Dennis for twenty-one yards. From the twenty he hit Joe Pettey on the eleven, but Martin's tackle smashed the ball loose and Versprille claimed it for Alabama. The Rebels wouldn't come close again. This football game was Alabama's.

And they were announcing in the press box that, for the first time in the history of any bowl, the Most Valuable Player in the 1964 Sugar Bowl was a placekicker. It was the crowning touch for the young man who would turn down professional offers to go on to make himself a physician.

"I could have gotten a little bonus and tried it," he said, "but it was going to get in the way of med school. I don't want to sound egotistical about it, but I knew that I could make it, but I would just be putting off something that was more important."

It was the kind of decision you'd expect from a quarterback who had a dream shattered along with his knee and then went out and made himself a new dream, which paid off handsomely for Alabama football—and never more so than in the Sugar Bowl following the snow.

If there was one flaw in the picture of happiness for Tim Davis as Paul Bryant knelt to lead his team in prayer after the victory, it was that Tim's dad hadn't been there to see it happen.

Alvin Davis, the first player recruited by young assistant Paul Bryant when he went to work for Frank Thomas in 1936, didn't get to New Orleans. The snow which covered that old city on the day before and wouldn't let travelers move had kept the father of the star at home.

9

A Time to Panic

February 20, 1960

His name was Jimmy Fibbe and he was from Frankfort, Kentucky, a slim-jim six feet, three inches tall, weighing no more than 170 pounds. He was the man—an engineer-to-be—who fired off two of the most telling shots in the history of Auburn basketball, and they rocketed the Tigers of 1960 to a Southeastern Conference championship they'd never have gotten without him.

An unlikely looking hero was Jimmy Fibbe, off an unlikely looking team that traveled the last mile to history always an inch from disaster. One false step and "Snow White" Joel Eaves's "Seven Dwarfs" would have been off the tightrope and into the soup.

Five times during the final month of the 1960 basketball season, Auburn's team went to the last minute to win. Twice the Tigers were in overtime and got out. They'd lost two games early in the year, and they couldn't lose any more—not if they were going to be champions.

The most pressure-packed moment of all was reserved for Fibbe of Frankfort, who had come to Auburn without anyone there ever having seen him play in high school. The insistent recommendation of an Auburn alumnus in Kentucky named P. I. Lowman put Fibbe there, a man for a moment. Other schools had sought him with scholarships, but not the University of Kentucky, which must have wished he'd have been somewhere else on the biggest night of all on Auburn's championship run.

They didn't look like champions, the little fellows coached by the tall, early gray Eaves, who moved on to become athletic director at Georgia but then was one of the most masterful tacticians U.S. college basketball had known. A brilliant student and a three-letter athlete at Auburn, Eaves was the same kind of coach. This team he coached was a natural for the name pinned on it by Bill Beckwith, an imaginative publicist. What else but Dwarfs? Henry Hart, the captain, stood six foot one, Ray Groover was an even six feet, Porter Gilbert was six foot one, and Jimmy Fibbe and David Vaughn were giants at six foot three. These were the starters. The sixth and seventh men were Bill Ross, six foot one, and Bayward McManus, five foot eight.

The other substitute was the team's giant. John Helmlinger stood six foot six. The story went that Helmlinger had suggested that in view of the team's nickname he could be carried as "Prince Charming," but Eaves, Hart, Groover, Gilbert, Fibbe, Vaughn, McManus, and Ross laughingly took care of that request.

Except for Helmlinger, who was a 200-pounder, the heavyweight of the team was Vaughn. David weighed 174 pounds.

Teams this size normally don't do much winning in big-league basketball. It's a grinding, punishing game, physically and mentally, and the Tigers of 1960 who would win the championship insisted, it seemed, on making it worse. They lived dangerously, ever more dangerously. Squeaker followed squeaker as the season grew older, and Auburn, Georgia Tech, and Kentucky fought it out down to the closing days. Every game was king-size by now, but there was one over all the rest, for the team, for the coach, for those who followed after them to record in print all that took place. Not surprisingly, *the* game was Kentucky on February 20, 1960, in the little sports arena at Auburn that had been an airplane hangar during World War II and had been converted nicely, but not spaciously. At most, 2,500 could crowd in.

Typically for Auburn, and with the aid of acoustics generally regarded as hideous by invading teams, 2,500 in the sports arena could make as much noise as 43,000 outside in Cliff Hare Stadium.

They had opened the doors at five on the wintry night the Wildcats came to see about stopping the small Auburn upstarts, and long before the teams got there the place was packed and jumping. Other games remained that had to be won, but here was the key. The crowd knew it as Eaves and his team and Adolph Rupp and his Wildcats knew it. Kentucky was 9-2 in Southeastern Conference play, and so was Auburn. Each would play fourteen games. This was the twelfth, an agonizing, tantalizing, terribly tense basketball game that seesawed from the beginning. Auburn leading, then Kentucky, and never a moment of ease for anyone playing or watching.

This was the year when Eaves's "shuffle" offense gained much prominence, although the Tigers did a great deal more freelancing than many opponents were aware, and they'd fast-break too. But mostly they went at it with deadly deliberation, waiting for the good shot, hitting most of the time around 50 percent. What many people didn't know was that this offense, which seemed almost to plod at times, had come about as a result of Eaves's careful planning. The coach knew, in the beginning, that most of it would be up to his starters, that physically they'd be outmanned anywhere. "We knew we had to get them as much rest as possible," he said. "We had patterns that let two men work and three men rest." The championship Auburn won was woven around one of these patterns, particularly.

So they went at it. Auburn scored first on a Fibbe layup; Kentucky struck back with a twenty-footer by Don Parsons. With seven minutes gone, Auburn led 10-7 after Groover swished in a short jump shot. A minute later Kentucky led 11-10 as Don Mills and Parsons scored again. The pattern was established. In the last minute of the first half, Kentucky took a three-point lead and went to intermission on top 32-29.

Start of the second half. Bang, bang, tied again. Gilbert drove for a bucket, Groover followed him, and it was cat-and-mouse once more.

Before the night was over, the score would be tied and the lead change hands forty times, and the crowd had nothing to do but go crazy, which it did.

They were into the last minute when Bill Lickert scored and Kentucky was in front 58–57. Fibbe drove, hooked, and Auburn led 59–58, and as the Wildcats came back down the floor only twenty seconds remained. Eight seconds were left when a twenty-footer by Kentucky's Larry Pursiful hit bottom, and this one belonged to Kentucky 60–59 as Eaves called his men to a time-out. The awful din now had been replaced by apprehensive silence. Rupp was gesturing wildly in the Kentucky huddle at one end of the floor. Eaves, all of it bottled up inside him, spoke quickly and firmly, and Auburn's players scattered. They had a plan.

"It was a screen roll," Eaves said, giving it its technical name as he played the game back in a quiet hour after he'd given up coaching and gone into the front office. "We overloaded to the left. Hart would get the ball while Fibbe screened and rolled, then Hart would pass to Fibbe. Fibbe could shoot and he had those good hands. He might have had the best hands of any college basketball player I ever saw."

The play never developed. The Tigers put it in motion, and Kentucky's Sid Cohen jumped into Fibbe as he came to the screening man. There was no question about the foul. Referee Toby Pace called it, and Jimmy Fibbe, junior from Frankfort, Kentucky, went to the line with one-and-one. Make the first and get a shot at the second.

Five seconds to play, and the battle had become Fibbe's alone. There was no one to help. What Fibbe looked at was as pressure-laden an assignment as any game might ever bring. Jack Nicklaus with a putt that would win the Masters could be close, perhaps, but what else?

There are eight men to help a baseball pitcher, and ten to go with a football quarterback. There is the physical presence of a contesting opponent to make muscles go in other games, but here was Fibbe, a ball and a basket, these and nothing more. For the instant, for Fibbe and the crowd, for the Kentucky and Auburn basketball players who waited, this had to be the biggest thing in all the world.

The pressure points: Jimmy Fibbe sinks second of two free throws—and Kentucky. (Courtesy Auburn University)

The skill was there. Fibbe had the good touch. An opponent might not defeat it, but the mind can be a treacherous enemy of the muscle. If a man couldn't think . . . but a man *must* think. Fibbe knew as he looked, and lifted the ball, then launched it straight, without arch, at the basket, which was the way he shot free throws.

One in, score tied.

Another in, Auburn ahead 61–60.

Now Kentucky came, and the screaming frenzy of the night wasn't done yet.

A long pass was out of bounds, knocked out by Auburn hands, and Cohen went to throw it in. He took three quick steps along the line, and Helmlinger had let his man, Allen Feldhaus, get free. Feldhaus drove at the basket, went in for a right-handed layup, but Helmlinger's desperate lunge blocked the shot. If the Kentuckian had gone from the left, Helmlinger might never have gotten there.

The ball came off the board, rolling loose for an instant. "I couldn't tell what was happening then, but you can see it in the pictures," Eaves recalled. "Hart and Cohen went for that thing like you'd go for a fumble in football. It squirted and another Kentucky player had it. Maybe time had run out, the film doesn't show the clock, but the Kentucky boy had it, six inches off the floor, and Hart reached, somehow, and knocked it away. That's the way he played. That's the way all of them played."

And that's the way Auburn defeated Kentucky 61–60, with Groover scoring twenty-two points, Fibbe seventeen, and Gilbert ten as the Tigers put up only thirty-six field goal attempts and got eighteen of them in. On Monday night the Tigers chilled Tennessee, and on the Saturday night following, in overtime, they put down Alabama at Montgomery for the championship. The winning basket was scored on a layup by Groover, with time almost gone, and he shot it off the pattern that Cohen had interrupted by fouling Fibbe the Saturday night before.

"That team," Eaves says now, "was amazing. Most of all, those boys were an illustration of how far intelligence and poise can take athletes, and intelligence is the first thing. They could shoot and pass, of course, but most of all that was an *intelligent* basketball team."

David Vaughn went on to become a physical therapist in Spartanburg, South Carolina; Gilbert, an engineer in Huntsville; Hart, with a large corporation in Atlanta; Ross, a high school coach there; McManus, athletic director for Jonesboro, Georgia, schools; and Groover, a doctor. In 1966 in Germany, playing basketball, Dr. Groover showed soldiers how it was. He scored forty points in a game. For Fibbe, a career in civil engineering followed basketball.

"We did rest them," Eaves said. "The last month, there were a lot of days when we didn't practice as long as forty-five minutes. We tinkered with zone defenses all year, anything to save the legs. They wore soft-soled shoes on trips, and played in ripple-soled shoes (a type worn much by college coaches with rubber ridges across the bottom). The short practices were as much to keep them from getting mentally tired as physically."

The most rested team that ever won a Southeastern Conference basketball championship will not be singled out by Eaves as "the best I ever had," though the record strongly suggests that this must be the case.

"You help the feelings of five or six boys and you hurt some others when you do a thing like that," Eaves said. "Every boy who played for me was important to me, and I just don't mean the ones with outstanding skill. A good boy, giving all he has, is just as important. The best things we've got are our young people. We had fine young men on our championship team. I'll be proud all of my life that I was there to coach them, and I don't think that once, in all of those tough, close games, they ever got scared. They never lost their poise. Just like Fibbe on the night we beat Kentucky."

Fibbe is the memory that must stay closest to those who were there the night Auburn cleared the highest hurdle on its way to the championship. These were the people who came leaping from the stands across the crowded press table while newspaper writers ducked and marveled.

One of them marveled some more when, in the midst of the multitude, he came upon Jimmy Fibbe and the pretty girl who had come to his side to share his triumph and make it sweeter with her happiness.

"I'm sure glad you made those shots," she told the hero of the hour.

"Well," Jimmy Fibbe said, and he had on a wide smile now, "I am, too."

Then the two of them were swept away in the wildly happy mob cheering the beating of Kentucky—which continues to be the utmost in Southeastern Conference basketball most any year.

10

When Is an Upset?

December 3, 1949

FOR THOSE WHO'LL PLAY IT, the morning of the game is a feeling to be remembered many years after; it's a mixture of anticipation ("Sure we'll win") and trepidation ("Will I do well?") and great pride at living in the center of a hurricane. Not many people can go there. They know you're there. They watch when you walk by and maybe they wish they walked there.

At Roebuck, on the eastern end of Birmingham, the Auburn football players came to December 3, 1949, like thousands before and thousands since. This doesn't change.

Travis Tidwell, Johnny Wallis, Tom Banks, Billy Tucker, Jim Mc-Gowen, Coker Barton, Chester Cline, Arnold Fagen, Ralph Pyburn, Virgil Willett, John Crolla, John Adcock, Max Autrey, Bobby Golden, Erskine Russell, and Bill Davis know because they were there in Coach Earl Brown's Auburn party that went for the bus at noon for the ride to Legion Field where Alabama waited, perhaps a little smugly.

Alabama had poleaxed Auburn 55–0 in 1948 when the state rivals resumed playing each other in football for the first time since 1907, when they had a fight and foolishly wouldn't get back together until the state legislature forced them to do so. There has never been another fight, incidentally. Just games, to be enjoyed and agonized over, but just games.

For the players, it's close to war; for the fans, it's a party, and the Auburn football players—quiet now and tense—found festivity surrounding them as they climbed aboard for the crosstown trip. Some fans had begun the party early, and there are times when bourbon doesn't bring out the best in football fans. These happy ones who would watch were waving fistfuls of bills and offering up bets as they approached the Auburn group.

"Give you twenty-five points, kid . . . Hey, War Eagle, this says you don't even score."

Later, some of the Auburn Tigers thought this might have been the final firing-up they needed for the big game at the end of the season. They'd show those people, they thought, after they'd shown them. The probability is that this little byplay had nothing whatsoever to do with the outcome of events shaping for the afternoon ahead at Legion Field, but it demonstrates the climate in which Auburn went to play Alabama on December 3, 1949. Auburn was a three-touchdown underdog. If Tidwell and Wallis and Banks and the rest of them thought they'd win this game, they represented a minority that included many of the citizens who'd go about Birmingham yelling "War Eagle!" when all of it was finished. The prevailing opinion was that this Auburn team didn't belong on the field with Alabama.

Alabama had Eddie Salem and Butch Avinger, Bill Cadenhead, Jack Brown, Red Lutz, Al Lary, Rebel Steiner, Mike Mizerany, Red Noonan, Tom Calvin, Pat O'Sullivan, Ed Holdnak, Larry Lauer, Herb Hannah, and Ed White, and Alabama was rolling. This was one of Red Drew's November teams. If you didn't get Alabama early in those years, forget it. The Crimson Tide had lost early to Tulane and to Vanderbilt, had been tied by Tennessee, then had blazed by Georgia, Georgia Tech, Southern Mississippi, and Florida.

Auburn had beaten Mississippi State, had tied Florida, Georgia, and Clemson. Mississippi, Georgia Tech, Tulane, and Vanderbilt had put the Tigers down, and that's how the table had been set for this feast that would pack Birmingham's Legion Field to its capacity then of forty-four thousand.

Sometimes in Alabama it's difficult to distinguish early December from mid-autumn. The day was beautiful blue, with a bit of a nip in the air and perfect for football, and this was the day when giant-killer Auburn went and got Alabama 14–13 in an upset that ranks with a 1942 victory over Rose Bowl–bound Georgia as possibly the two greatest such in all the history of War Eagles, who lived then with a tradition that they were most to be feared when they were underdogs. They liked to be underdogs, lurking, ambushing, springing a trap. On December 3, 1949, the trap was magnificent.

Tidwell, the quarterback from Birmingham's Woodlawn, who guided it, wouldn't take that view along later when he'd been to pro ball and returned home to a successful business career.

"We were as good a football team as they were," he said. "We wanted to win a little more. We'd been hearing about that 55–0 for a long time."

The year before, the score had been 7–0 in the second quarter when quarterback Tidwell—an Auburn freshman sensation when he came home from the war in 1946, then broke an ankle in 1947 playing baseball and wasted much of two seasons—got hurt. Tidwell had listened to the rout from a hospital bed.

"Look back at our record," Tidwell said. "Tulane, which was winning the conference championship that year, beat us 14–6 with a sixty-five-yard touchdown run by Eddie Price, and we had a touchdown called back that Jocko Norton scored on a punt return. We had Georgia 20–6 with six minutes left to play and let them get away to tie us 20–20. Clemson was 20–20, too. It sounds funny, maybe, with our overall record, but by the time we got to Alabama we thought we could beat anybody. We weren't scared when we went out there; we weren't scared of it a bit."

The late arrivers still were stumbling over legs and causing necks to stretch for a view of the field when this fact of life became apparent.

Alabama won the toss, Captain Cadenhead versus Captain Pyburn and Alternate Captain Barton of Auburn. The Tigers kicked off, and here was a battle, here was the way it would be. Red Noonan ran at the line twice and gained nothing. Ed Salem lost a yard. Avinger punted forty-one yards, Jim McGowen quick-kicked back, and Alabama was back on its twenty. The first quarter would produce only one first down, put together by Bimbo Melton and Noonan, and here was a smashing, bruising football game. No one thought any longer that it would be easy for anyone.

As the second quarter came on, Alabama had been kicked back to its thirteen yard line by McGowen. Now, the fireworks, the sudden, dramatic explosion that put underdog Auburn on top. It was a pass from the sixteen on second down by Salem, aimed at Al Lary in the flat, and Wallis, the chunky halfback from Birmingham's Ensley, played the ball perfectly. This pass never came close to a receiver. Wallis took it at the eighteen, going full-speed toward the goal. If he had gambled, he had won. An instant and he was over and, most improbably to most of them there, Auburn led 6–0. Billy Tucker, quarterback and placekicker, converted for 7–0. Forty-five seconds of the period had been used up.

One exchange of punts after the kickoff and Alabama was driving back, giving better than it got, intent on getting this surprising situation in hand. From its thirty-seven the Tide wheeled to first down on Auburn's thirteen, with Al Lary running fifteen yards on an end-around, Melton scooting for fifteen and seven. A fifteen-yard penalty helped.

Down close, it was nothing doing. Calvin made two yards, but Melton was thrown down five yards behind the line. Bob Cochran passed for three yards to Avinger. On fourth down a Salem pass to Calvin was incomplete, and Auburn took the football back on its thirteen yard line. The bands were getting out of their seats now and moving down toward the sidelines for the halftime marching and music. Time was fleeting.

McGowen had a clutch punt ready for the occasion. It was a forty-seven-yarder, but Salem—a big-play man for three varsity seasons at Alabama—shook his way loose for a thirty-nine-yard return to the Tiger thirty-three, and this time the Tide wasn't stopping. Working from the Notre Dame box, shifting, Salem sent White left and the end-around was good again for twenty yards. Then the former Ramsay-of-Birmingham star took care of the remainder. Avinger and Calvin led Salem around right end, thirteen yards to the end zone. Salem converted, and it was 7–7 at intermission. They were back where they'd started, all even.

Auburn, which had scored its touchdown the easy way, was geared for something more when the second half began. Quickly, Tidwell led his team to Alabama's twenty-nine before the first Tiger drive of the game was ground to a halt by Elliott Speed and Red Lutz. Avinger punted out, and when Holdnak jumped on a fumble on the Auburn forty-nine, opportunity was knocking again for the favorites. The door apparently was caving in when Salem hit White with a pass to the thirty-two, but this one wasn't for Alabama. The next Salem pass was picked off by Brownie Flourney, who got it back up to the Auburn twenty-nine, late in the third quarter, and it was from here that the Tigers hammered for the points that would carry the day.

Tidwell, Davis, and McGowen were the workmen as Auburn ground it out through the closing minutes of the third quarter, and it was McGowen striking for nine to the twenty on the first play of the fourth quarter. Tidwell, masterful leader, had his bunch on fire. In the west stands, where Auburn's tickets were sold, now they were beginning to think "Maybe," and they stood and screamed. That was getting to be a pretty delirious place down in the shadows of the afternoon.

Now Jim Jeffers, a sophomore fullback, struck for three and McGowen for three more. Tidwell slid through the right side for seven, and Max Autrey was there to help him when the ball was jolted loose.

Travis Tidwell (11) sees daylight against the Tide. Later he, not the coach, got the victory ride. (Courtesy Auburn University)

Auburn was on the eleven, and Tidwell sent Bill Davis wide, then cutting back over ground blocked clean ahead of him, and he scored. Tucker kicked again. Fourteen to seven now.

Here came Alabama! Melton ran the kickoff out twenty-eight yards to his forty-four. Melton made two yards. Salem, hemmed up while trying to pass, got out for twenty-one. Lary tried the end-around twice, for three and for five, and Calvin powered through the middle for four and a first down.

Not yet, however, not for Alabama. Salem picked up five on first down, but Calvin lost a yard. Salem came back for four, but it was fourth down and two. The end-around wouldn't work at all this time. White had the ball and made nothing, and Auburn had saved the homestead again.

McGowen kicked out. Alabama cranked up once more from its forty-seven with a little less than four minutes showing on the clock, and now the most the Tide could hope to salvage was a tie. Melton ran three, Salem six, Calvin ten, but Salem lost ten trying to pass. Now there had to be another throw, and this one was dead on target from Salem to Melton, who took the ball on the ten and went to the three before Wallis caught him. Salem ran two, then Calvin cashed the touchdown, and here it was. If it had been fifteen years later, Alabama might have gone for two, undoubtedly would have felt compelled to go for two, but all there could be in 1949 was a kick for one more point from the steady Salem, and that would leave it 14–14.

So they huddled and Salem was testing his leg, backward, forward, warming up while Butch Avinger called the play. They lined up; Jack Brown got the snap from center, set the ball down, and Salem's kick was away, tumbling to the right of the goalposts, off line, no good.

"He missed it, he missed it, he missed it," an elderly gentleman on the west side said over and over again in front of a sportswriter out on a football-watching holiday. He knew, all of the crowd knew, that the story had been written, the battle was done, done, done.

Alabama's onside kickoff—a last, desperate hope—was claimed by Auburn, and Tidwell killed the clock, quarterback-sneaking three times into the line, and that's the way it ended. Auburn 14, Alabama 13, on December 3 of the year of 1949 at Legion Field in Birmingham, Alabama.

Significantly, the man the Auburn players hurried for to give a ride upon their shoulders when the game was over wasn't Earl Brown, the coach. The Tigers lifted Tidwell up, and there are people who will tell you to this day that more than any one man, Travis Tidwell was responsible for that Auburn Tiger football triumph.

The next year, Tidwell had gone to the New York Giants, and Auburn lost ten straight football games, including the last one to Alabama 34–0. Earl Brown's three-year career at Auburn had ended. His teams had won three games in all that time. In 1951, with Ralph Jordan coaching, Auburn had won three as soon as it had played three, and a new time had come. Suddenly, Auburn wasn't an underdog as it had been before. Now Auburn was supposed to win, and did, and no one challenged its football players on the mornings of the games when the boys with the stern-man faces went out to play.

Auburn found out how nice it feels to be a favorite, though you'd never convince Travis Tidwell, Jim McGowen, Billy Tucker, and Erskine Russell that it was otherwise on December 3, 1949, in Birmingham. "Upset? That was no upset," said Tidwell. "We knew we were going to win," and they sure did.

11

Prelude to a Grand Slam

June 7, 1917

THERE MAY BE MORE THAN A few in the wild, whooping new generation of followers after golf who don't really know about Bobby Jones.

They march in Arnie's Army at all of the places where the PGA tour takes golfers in the search for gold that now has become the game's big thing, or cheer one of half a hundred brilliant shot-makers.

The U.S. Amateur, the British Amateur—what are they? Arnie has won more than a million dollars at Pensacola and Doral, at Phoenix, Tucson, Greensboro, Dallas, and New Orleans, and in the Masters, and all over the world.

At the Masters they might have seen Jones, confined to a wheel-chair, an invalid physically but not in the heart, and maybe they linger to hear what he says at the presentation ceremonies when the long four days are done. Maybe they hurry off, for it's a long drive back to the places they came from.

They should know that the Masters *is* Robert T. Jones, and Cliff Roberts too; that this golf course where it is played, laid out lovingly between the Georgia pines where the wind swoops low to clutch at shots many days, is his golf course. The wistful beauty of Augusta National, scene every April of the Masters, has in it, I think, much of the romance of the game Bobby Jones loved and played best in a time when professionals were teachers, not tourists, and gentleman amateurs were the players in tournaments. It is not the same game now which Bobby Jones's memories embrace. In many ways it's better, but it's not the same, which is mostly what this is all about.

Robert Tyre Jones first found a golf club in his hand when he was six years old. His father had put it there at the East Lake Country Club in Atlanta, which had three golf courses—country club courses, if you will—at that time. Only the well-to-do played the game. There might not have been a dozen kids throughout the city who had ever seen a golf ball hit or ever held a golf club in hand.

Golf was nothing except genteel, and sports pages knew little of it, being more taken with boxing matches and baseball games in that day, which was 1908 when the United States was flexing its muscles and growing mighty over the world, and the old wounds left from the Civil War were being healed by time, though many who had fought it couldn't forget.

In 1930, when Bobby Jones was twenty-eight years old, he won the British Amateur, the British Open, the U.S. Amateur, and the U.S. Open for a Grand Slam that put him in the front seat for a ticker tape parade down the streets of New York City, and sports pages saved their biggest type for headlines carrying his name. Bobby Jones had made golf that big, and it would do nothing except grow in this land that loves games.

More than any other man, Jones was the beginning.

He won everything in sight. Then he quit in 1930 because the time had come for him to get busy with his law practice. Golf was for fun on weekends. The day would never come when Robert T. Jones, barrister, would desert his old love completely. He couldn't have if he'd wanted to because this was one of those matches made in heaven, starting when Bobby was six and his father took him to the temptress who would win him, put a golf club in his hand.

Bobby Jones in Birmingham: from a brilliant victory here, he
went on to the Grand Slam. (Courtesy *Birmingham News*)

This was what brought Bobby Jones to the Roebuck Springs Country Club, out past Birmingham's East Lake, in the early summer of
1917, while World War I tore at Europe. The Atlantan had won an
invitational tournament here the year before, and another at the Birmingham Country Club, but this precocious youngster had never
won a big one. He'd only a year earlier gotten his first pair of long
pants, because boys didn't come by the first pair easily. It was the kind

of thing parents talked about in the night after children were asleep, the taking of that kind of a step.

Fifty years later, Jones would remember the "magnificent swimming pool, with the ice-cold water" at the Roebuck Springs Country Club. He would remember that more, in fact, than many details of what happened here where the Southern Amateur Championship was being settled in 1917, when Bobby was just fifteen years old.

He was a youngster having a world of fun, mostly, and he wouldn't have been awed a bit by a Southern Amateur, because he had won two matches in the National Amateur in 1916 before the defending champion put him out in the third round.

Bobby Jones began the Southern Amateur on June 7, 1917, at Roebuck by putting out one of his elders, T. M. Mayes, seven and six, and he came back in the afternoon of this Thursday against Alan Bush, the defending champion. It was tougher, but Jones liked the golf course and he was playing well. He eliminated the champ, three and two, and now they were beginning to say around the clubhouse that "Little Bobby" just might win this thing.

The semifinals sent him against Thomas Wheelock, a seventeen-year-old New Orleans boy, described in the papers as "the surprise of the tourney." Jones got him, four and three, and that brought him to Saturday, June 9, and the thirty-six-hole final with Lewis Jacoby of Dallas, New Orleans, and Charlotte, North Carolina.

Picking Jones to win in Saturday morning's *Age-Herald*, sports columnist Henry Vance wrote, "He's playing the best game of his life, has taken on a confidence in his work that stands him in good stead. . . .

"If Jones does not quit the game the victor, all Atlanta will doll herself in mourning tomorrow morning and Sunday will be a day of weeping and wailing and gnashing of molars."

Vance noted further, "A gallery of 500 is following the two men and Birmingham is evidencing more interest in today's battle than any golf match ever staged within the confines of Jones Valley."

As it developed, one part of Henry Vance's confident prophecy missed by a mile. A downpour swept over the course an hour before finalists Jones and Jacoby were to go off at ten, and a stiff breeze was left behind as a souvenir. The enormous gallery of five hundred did not materialize. The course was water-soaked. The attack of the elements might have bothered Jacoby. The Georgia boy couldn't have cared less as he drilled his tee shot on the first hole twenty yards ahead of his older opponent, came across the creek intersecting the fairway on his second, into the middle of the green, and two-putted for a par four, which beat Jacoby's five.

The "Grand Slam" was beginning; the headlines to go around the world were starting on a wet, windy June day on the outskirts of Birmingham.

Hitting into the teeth of a small gale, Jones was fifty yards ahead of his opponent with his drive on the second. Jones's pitch was within three feet of the pin. He missed the birdie, but par was good enough to win again from the nervous Jacoby.

Listen to the future and hear the cheers thirteen years away for British Amateur, British Open, U.S. Amateur, U.S. Open. Bobby Jones is on his way.

Jones went, straight as a string off the tee, getting his putts down, magnificent on a wretched day, to three-up at the turn, to five-up after eleven, and that's how it stood when they went to lunch after the first eighteen.

The youngster might have been dazzled a bit by the ease of it all. Jacoby struck back as the afternoon round began. He won No. 1 with a bogey five when Bobby found all kinds of trouble for a double-bogey six. Jacoby's par won No. 2, and par was good enough for the Texan, North Carolinian, Louisianian again on No. 3. Jones's overwhelming lead in the match had now been reduced to two-up.

Wave of the future? Nothing else but. Right here, fifteen-year-old Bobby Jones demonstrated part of what it was that would one day make him king of it all. He birdied No. 4 to go three-up and reestablished once and for all who was commander of this show. When they headed to the back nine for the second time, the fifteen-year-old was five-up and winging.

He closed out the match, six and four, with his par four on the fourteenth, and Jacoby shook the hand of the chunky fifteen-year-old from Atlanta, a senior at Tech High School, who had let him escape from complete annihilation, but not by too much.

O. B. Keeler, the Atlanta golf writer who would travel 120,000 wonderful miles watching Jones play golf, rejoicing in his triumphs, being saddened by his reverses, might have been in the gathering in Roebuck Springs clubhouse shortly after six o'clock.

Trophies were presented to winners of all flights, it was reported in the Sunday *Birmingham News,* which had headlined the match, "Dazzling Skill of Georgia Star Bewilders Texan," and subheaded, "Handicapped by Deluge of Rain, a Water-Soaked Course and Fish-Tailed Wind, Jones Startles All by Brilliant Work."

The end of the story of Jones's first major tournament triumph carried this note:

"Young Bob Jones thanked the club and officials for their courtesy during the tournament and declared that Roebuck was the best course he had ever played, and that the greens committee should be collectively and individually thanked for their work in making the course splendid, for he had won the championship through their efforts."

Robert Tyre Jones didn't need instruction in diplomacy, either.

The door had swung open wide for him. Everything that an amateur could win in golf was about to be his. He won the Open in 1923 but couldn't go to the Walker Cup matches in England because he was in school at Harvard. He won his first National Amateur in 1924 and took it again in 1925. There was half of a Grand Slam in 1926, the American Open and the British Open, and the stage was being set, gradually, awaiting the time when Bobby Jones at his peak would win everything, then say, "Good-bye. It has been wonderful."

The Birmingham chapter has been overlooked in much latter-day chronicling of the wonder of Bobby Jones, but it's part of the record of an immortal, and it needed to be set down firmly and fully. Anyone who can claim a piece of Bobby Jones shouldn't let the opportunity get away.

It's history that the name which would grow to mean more to golf than any other, the name that Arnold Palmer and Jack Nicklaus and Masters winners speak almost with reverence, won the first time, the first big time, at Roebuck Springs with the magnificent swimming pool and the ice-cold water.

The Country Club has been a municipal course for many years, but the creek still intersects the first fairway. The swimming pool has disappeared, though the springs around Roebuck still gush as icy and crystal clear as in 1917 when Jones came here to win the Southern Amateur.

There is a paragraph in Bobby Jones's book, *Golf Is My Game,* that a sportswriter must include somewhere. It was in the course of a tribute to Keeler, one of the great early ones in my business, that Jones wrote:

"To gain any sort of fame it isn't enough to do the job. There must be someone to spread the news. If fame can be said to attach to one because of his proficiency in the inconsequential performance of striking a golf ball, what measure of it I have enjoyed has been due in large part to Keeler and his gifted typewriter."

At fifteen, he stood in the clubhouse at Roebuck, fresh-faced and serious, and told all the people there they had the best golf course he had ever played, and he said "Thank you," and he always did. He kept on saying it to golf with the Masters.

12

Paid in Full

January 1, 1965

THE FLIPPING OF THE HALF DOLLAR, the introduction of the players, the rendition of the National Anthem (with fireworks), the scalping of the tickets, and all other pregame ritual had been attended to. Now the Orange Bowl would offer the first night game in its history, national champion Alabama against Texas. It was January 1, 1965, in Miami.

There had been a slight rain, following an afternoon downpour, but the wetness had gone away to wait until a halftime visit for dousing all the lovely, brightly colored floats.

A warm wind blew, tugging at majorettes' skirts and banners and things. The night was alive with anticipation, loaded with promise. The minute before kickoff had come. Players ran to take their places, and the roar of the multitude rose to greet them. This is the time that somehow you always must remember. Great calm, quieting to a murmur, then the storm. That's the way all football games begin.

On the Alabama side of the field, Paul Bryant had shed his raincoat and his sport jacket and replaced his checkered hat with an old Alabama baseball cap. Sartorial splendor had been sacrificed to the urgency of the hour, and comfort.

Now, the coach moved alongside Jim Goostree, the fine Crimson Tide trainer, and Alabama's coach had a last-second question.

"Can Joe play?" Bryant asked.

"Yessir," said Goostree. "Joe can play."

How Joe played and the way he played with one bum leg, and finally looking for receivers from eyes blurred with pain, made an epic for the history of the Orange Bowl that long and steaming night in Miami.

It wasn't a game Alabama would win—lost only by inches—and there were many tremendous days and nights in the college career of Joe Willie Namath of Beaver Falls, Pennsylvania, that must look better in the record books. But this is the football game that belongs in this book, because quite simply, it was greater than the days against Georgia Tech and Georgia and Tennessee, when Namath was winning pitcher.

Too much to-do is made over the quality of courage in athletics. There is a demand, certainly, but nothing to equal that of a kid being shot at on a battlefield or in a Pacific jungle. What's often called courage could better be defined in athletics as skill, and perhaps a high threshold of pain. It hurts, but most of the time only for a little while.

In this Orange Bowl, on that night, Joe Namath did what he did on guts, plus ability, and he will be remembered for it far more than any of the Texans who could go off celebrating, late in the almost-tropical night, because they had won 21–17, had beaten the No. 1 team in the nation. They didn't talk of Texas too much across the country after that one. They didn't talk of Alabama too much, either. They talked of Joe Namath.

This was the boy who had come to be a Crimson Tidesman after he'd missed, by no more than a point in an exam, getting into Maryland. The second pass he threw as a sophomore was a touchdown. He became an instant star. Then, late in his junior season, with a Miami

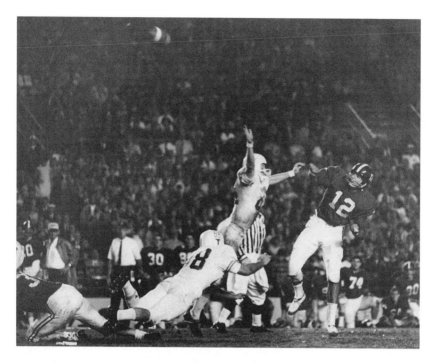

On one good leg, Namath fires against onrushing Texans—and pays a debt to Alabama. (Courtesy *Birmingham News*)

game and the Sugar Bowl with Ole Miss remaining, he had been suspended for breaking training rules.

The way he fought back the next spring, to win his teammates, to reclaim his place out front, was loaded with courage and determination, too. In September of 1964, Namath was the quarterback, surely headed for a brilliant senior season. He had it all going for him.

Georgia was first, and the 31–3 victory Namath engineered at Tuscaloosa was a masterpiece. Then Alabama decked Tulane 36–6 and Vanderbilt 24–0. This show was on the road. On Saturday, October 10, at Tuscaloosa it became something else for the quarterback. While Alabama was defeating North Carolina State 21–0, he rolled out, cut back on a routine running play, and his right knee buckled beneath him. It would never be the same again.

Namath and Steve Sloan were dividing the duty the rest of the undefeated way to No. 1 in the nation, and on to the Orange Bowl. This would be the end for Joe. Next, the pros, and the layoff after the Auburn game that wrapped up the season, seemed to work wonders. There was no limp, no trace of the knee injury when Bryant took his squad into Miami.

Then it happened again. Monday before the game at the Miami baseball park. Routine work, mostly running around. Suddenly, Namath was down again, his face contorted by the pain of the knee that had deserted him once more. As they carried him to the dressing room there was little hope, anywhere, that he could play Friday night. Put on a suit, yes. Compete? Impossible.

"I'll play," Namath insisted that afternoon. And he kept on insisting, but Sloan was the quarterback when the referee's hand came down and David Ray ran forward to kick off the 1965 Orange Bowl for Alabama.

It was getting along in the first quarter when Namath made his first appearance. This one gave no sign of what was to come. A fumble recovery at the Texas forty-three by Cecil Dowdy had given Alabama its first good chance in the still-scoreless game. Namath came in on third down and threw an incomplete pass, then David Ray missed a thirty-six-yard field goal.

Now, lightning struck. On second down, Ernie Koy, the big Texas fullback, crashed through right tackle, cut back, and found himself wide open for a seventy-nine-yard touchdown run. David Conway's placement made it 7–0.

Five minutes into the second quarter and Jim Hudson, the second-string Texas quarterback, hit George Sauer Jr. with a sixty-nine-yard touchdown pass. It was 14–0. Now the hobbling Namath, a quarterback with one leg, took over for good for Alabama.

From the thirteen, after the kickoff, Namath passed twenty-five yards to Ray Perkins, then hit him for eight, and Les Kelley ran a first down. It was Namath to Wayne Trimble for eleven yards, Namath to Tommy Tolleson for fifteen to the Texas twenty-three. Namath to

Wayne Cook made fourteen, and Namath to Trimble was a touchdown. Ray's kick made it 14–7 with 4:34 left in the half.

Texas stormed back, all the way to the Alabama twenty-eight, with time running out, and here big, freak trouble struck the Tide. With the Longhorns stopped, Conway was in to try a field goal and Creed Gilmer, the great little defensive end, got in front of the ball. Ray scooped up the blocked kick, running toward the Texas end of the field, but he never got a good clutch on it, lost it back to the Longhorns, and Texas had new life, presently a touchdown. From the Alabama thirty-eight, the Longhorns went to the thirteen on a twenty-five-yard penalty for holding downfield, and Koy hammered on in, scoring from a foot out, and Conway's kick finished the Texas scoring twenty-one seconds before intermission. It was 21–7.

Alabama kicked off, starting the second half, presently had the football on its thirty-seven after a punt, and here came Namath. Texas didn't know what to do about Namath, who could only pass, couldn't run at all. If the Longhorns rushed, he hit them with a quickie. If they didn't rush, he'd find a man long. In nine plays from the thirty-seven, crippled Joe Namath got another touchdown. First, a nine-yard pass to Tommy Tolleson and a couple of short runs. Then a fourth-and-eight completion to Ray Perkins for first down on the Texas twenty, and right back the same way, twenty more through the air to Perkins for six points. Ray kicked and it was 21–14 with only six minutes of the third quarter used up.

As the period ended, Namath's passes to Cook, to Ray Ogden, and to Trimble had Alabama on the Texas ten. A third-down pass missed, and on the second play of the fourth quarter Ray kicked a twenty-seven-yard field goal to cut the Texas margin to 21–17. A touchdown would win for Alabama over the stunned Longhorns, and Namath had plenty of time.

Texas couldn't move with the kickoff. Alabama took a punt and punted back. It was a desperate struggle now. An interception by Jimmy Fuller opened the door for the Tide nine minutes and fifty-three seconds from the end. Here it was. Go and get it.

Fuller grabbed the ball on the Texas thirty-four, and Namath right away passed to Ogden for seventeen yards, then to Steve Bowman for first down on the six. Bowman hit up the middle for four yards to the two, and Alabama had three downs to cover six feet. Alabama was seventy-two inches away from a triumphant end to one of the most amazing comebacks ever put together in any football game.

On second down, Bowman made a foot. On third down, he gained a yard. Now, it was two feet—twenty-four inches to go. Who would take it? Namath would. He came from the huddle behind Gaylon McCollough. The snap was quick, and the lines met, and there are people who will swear to this day that Namath crossed over. After discussion, the officials decided finally that he was down on the one foot line.

Texas kicked out. Namath was intercepted. Alabama took the ball back, finally, for one last effort from its thirty-one with a little more than two minutes left. Now, Namath couldn't see because a finger had been stuck in his eye, but one-eyed and one-legged, he had passed Alabama over to the Texas forty-one when the game ended.

The television people went for Namath. He had thrown for 255 yards. He, from the losing side, was a unanimous press-box choice as Most Valuable Player. Watching from the press box, you saw Namath break away from his TV escort once, go to Bryant, then come back again for the final pictures of the night.

Someone asked the coach about it in the dressing room, and he said, "Joe asked me to get him out of there. He said he didn't think he ought to go out there. He said he wasn't a winner."

That was typical Namath. Bryant was typical, too. People came to the dressing room looking for controversy over the fourth-down play on which Namath thought he scored, and most of his buddies did, too. Alabama's coach shrugged off a suggestion that the football took virtually no Alabama bounces.

"You make your own bounces," he said. "When you can't move the ball two yards on three downs, you can't win," and that's all he ever would say about it, except that he called the fourth-down play, though Namath might tell you differently if you asked that superstar of the New York Jets.

Namath wouldn't admit, ever, that the bowl game that will always be remembered for what he did was a good one for him. "We didn't win," he said the next morning, but he was prepared to smile a little now for he was on the way to the press conference where the Jets' Sonny Werblin was prepared to announce that Alabama's one-legged quarterback, who would soon have a knee operation, had been signed to a contract calling for more than $400,000 in salary and bonus for three years. It was, at that time, the richest contract ever signed by a professional athlete.

Namath had the knee operation and went on to become the American Football League's Rookie of the Year, a starter from the fourth game of the season on, the big, big gate attraction the struggling AFL had needed. He sold out everywhere, because he threw footballs like no one this league ever had seen before.

There was another knee operation, and the left knee came to trouble him also. Pass rushers knew that Namath couldn't run away, couldn't elude them, but he threw so quickly, so well that the pros couldn't get any more done with him than Texas could in the Orange Bowl, which was Joe Willie's finest hour.

Joe Willie Namath wouldn't let hurting stop him. The headlines spilled across him, and in his first three years he became as famous off the field as on it. He'd grow a beard now and then, and he let his hair grow long in the best New York style, too. The ladies loved him, and he found their company pleasant also. He was a "swinger," and the image was promoted by Werblin, the show-business man who reaped a golden harvest in publicity from his investment.

The close of the 1967 season was typically Namath. He was closing in on passing records when Ben Davidson of Oakland broke his cheekbone in the next-to-last game, but he went to work, injury or no, against San Diego on the closing Sunday. He became, that day, the only quarterback in all of professional history to gain more than four thousand yards throwing the football in a single season. While the

Jets were beating the Chargers, 42–31, he hit eighteen of twenty-six for 343 yards and four touchdowns. The final record-breaking total was 4,007, and it must have been a tremendous afternoon to see.

But if Namath quarterbacks for twenty years more, he won't capture a nation as he did in the Orange Bowl on Friday night, January 1, 1965. It was once-in-a-lifetime, a privilege to watch as Joe Willie Namath of Beaver Falls, Pennsylvania, paid in full measure for all that Alabama football had given him. Texas won. So did Joe.

13

7–7, Favor Howard

September 28, 1935

THE NAME OF THE SCHOOL WAS Howard College then, and it stood on a piece of ground in East Lake in Birmingham that looked immense to a freshman just in from the country. Dr. T. V. Neal was the president, but Major Harwell Davis would be there shortly to start this Baptist liberal arts college on its way to becoming Samford University on a beautiful campus green in the valley below Shades Mountain.

Behind Main Building, adjacent to Causey Gymnasium, which was said to be the most magnificent in the area, was Berry Field. The football players dressed in Causey Gym, then hoofed it in their stockinged feet across the pavement to lace up the cleated shoes for practice on Berry Field, and practice could be heard all the way over to the Pi Kappa Phi house in the woods beyond. The voices of Head Coach Billy Bancroft and Assistant Ray Davis rose shrilly when football players were to be scolded, or praised, and they had a good carrying quality. Voices are important in coaching football.

This was the year 1935, and Howard College football was important at Howard, and Birmingham paid some attention too. The annual season-ending game between Howard and Birmingham-Southern drew crowds of fifteen thousand and up, and it was bitter rivalry. Sportswriters at the *Birmingham News* and the *Birmingham Age-Herald* called this game "The Battle of the Marne," after that World War I inferno, which was still close enough to be remembered vividly on Armistice Day when the veterans paraded.

Howard College football players were mostly from little places, though they were given room, board, and tuition, and some had had tryouts at schools like Alabama or Auburn or Tennessee before coming to the less demanding security of a Howard scholarship. Some never got a look at a larger school, because the scouring of the countryside for athletes by college talent scouts wasn't the highly organized business it is now. The young men came to Howard and played, studied some, and generally did very well for themselves. It was a good life in hard times. The Hoover Depression—you couldn't call it anything else in Democratic Alabama—was easing up, but the Howard football player who came with two suits of clothes would likely be rumored a rich man's son.

On the starting Howard College team of 1935, Penny Penrod, the second-string fullback and placekicker, was from somewhere in Oklahoma, and Dan Snell, who died in World War II, was from Erie, Pennsylvania, but the rest of them were Alabama boys, several of them from Birmingham.

Norman Cooper, the center, came from Rogersville, and Tracy Burger, who played right guard, was from Etowah County. One tackle, Pat Harrison, was from Thomasville, and the other, Harry Johnston, was from Phillips in Birmingham. Adrian McKenzie from Northport played a lot of tackle that year, too. Paul Davis, from Cherokee, was at left halfback.

Ewing Harbin, the triple-threat left halfback, was a Shades Cahaba boy, and Glenn Hearn, the right halfback, who would go on to become mayor of Huntsville after an FBI career, was born and brought up in Albertville. Raymond Christian, more recently Dr. Raymond Christian, superintendent of Birmingham city schools, was the fullback, and he was from Northport. Wilton Batson, the left-handed, redheaded end, came from Bessemer.

Except when the old-timers get together at Samford reunions and occasionally at a Samford football game in Seibert Stadium, most of their names are not names much talked about in the history of Alabama sports. Cooper went on to become a fine pro center at Brooklyn, then coached at Vanderbilt, Kansas, and Louisiana State before moving home to get into the business world, but the others went railroading, teaching, and the like.

A time and a place found them together, however, and made them part of a memorable hour, which came on September 28 in 1935, a football year begun notably on January 1 by Alabama and Howell and Hutson in the Rose Bowl at Pasadena. On September 28, this Howard team coached by Bancroft and Davis and Roy Fayet, better known as Pooch, with Dewitt (Maw) Dunn, the trainer, took on the champions of the Rose Bowl in Denny Stadium, and the 7–7 tie they brought away was as sweet as any victory any team ever won. It was headline news in the *New York Times*. It was, that September, the most shocking football development in the United States of football. Howard tie Alabama? It couldn't happen. But it did.

The Crimson Tide of the 1935 season wasn't quite the one that had been to the bowl. Howell and Hutson were gone, for one big thing, and so were some others. Riley Smith, the all-American quarterback, was hurt and couldn't play on September 28 when Alabama came to its season-opening breather with the little school from Birmingham. But Alabama and Howard, Frank Thomas and Billy Bancroft, were different worlds, still. This was for getting the Tide ready for Tennessee, for Mississippi State—which had beaten Howard 19–6 a week before—and for Georgia, Kentucky, Clemson, Georgia Tech, George Washington, and Vanderbilt.

It was a little story later that Thomas and Red Drew, his assistant, had told Bancroft seriously during the summer, "Except for Riley Smith, we'd trade squads with you." Bancroft's reaction was, "You're pulling my leg," but he knew he had a sound football team, as big as

Alabama's, strong, and not scared of anybody. The way Thomas and Drew were supposed to have told it to Coach Bill of Howard was, "Your four guards are better than ours, and your center Cooper is twice as good as anybody we've got (which he probably was), and your four tackles are better than our four and your four ends are better." One of the ends who has laughed at the story since was a fellow from Arkansas they called "Bear."

So, the way it happened, Bancroft loaded his boys up Saturday morning in East Lake and they bused down to Tuscaloosa for tea and toast before the game. Somebody figured out in later years that steak was better and likely to put much more strength in a young man for a tough two hours, but in 1935 it was hot tea and toast. The Howard Bulldogs had theirs at the McLester Hotel, then went on to the stadium to dress. This was two hours, maybe a little more, before game time.

Bancroft and Davis left them there, all ready except for shoulder pads, sitting in the dressing room, looking at one another, and all the funny guys on one of the most relaxed football squads ever suddenly had nothing to say. The quiet comes now and then across one of the places where athletes wait, and it's ominous, and that's what was building that September 28 in the visitors' dressing room. There would have been no way for Frank Thomas, master psychologist, to have convinced his troops at the other end of the stadium that any sort of a storm was brewing, of course. The players knew what Howard was for, and that would have been that.

They kicked it off, and all of forty-five hundred were there to watch Alabama breeze into the new season, as Tennessee would the same day against Southwestern, Georgia against Mercer, Georgia Tech against Oglethorpe. This was warm-up day all around the Southeastern Conference, then in its second season after breaking away from the old, unwieldy Southern Conference.

Except in Denny Stadium it was Howard driving, not Alabama. In the first quarter, that was Howard putting on a drive to Alabama's six-yard line which only personal heroics by linebacker Kay Francis

Warm-up for a surprise warm-up at Tuscaloosa: Howard's Christian, Hearn, Browne, and Harbin. (Courtesy Samford University)

stopped short. Cooper, the linebacker, and Harrison and McKenzie and Johnston and Snell weren't letting the Tide move the football.

Normalcy apparently had returned early in the second quarter when Joe Riley found Jimmy Walker open for a touchdown pass. Riley threw and Walker caught, but Bear Bryant was offside and they called it back. Alabama struck again, quickly, from Howard's forty-six. Jimmy Angelich got fourteen yards in two cracks at center, and Rudy Rhordanz got through left tackle to the Bulldog twenty-seven. Two shots by sophomore halfback Joe Kilgrow put the ball on the Howard four. Angelich went in from there, Jim Whatley kicked the seventh point, and they went back to the dressing rooms at halftime with Alabama leading 7–0 and, so said the newspaper accounts, apparently not too much stirred up over the situation yet.

They sparred through a scoreless third quarter, and someone in the press box said, "Alabama hasn't come home from California yet."

Pushed back by a sixty-four-yard Joe Riley punt in the fourth quarter, Howard was in danger again as Alabama drove deep, but Percy Yeargen, in at end, and Cooper poured through to get Riley for a five-yard loss and the Bulldogs took the ball at their sixteen. A first down later came the break, the big one, that Howard had to have. This was a thirty-seven-yard penalty, half the distance to the goal as the rules had it, and Howard lined up with a first down on the Tide thirty-seven. Herbert Browne and Wilson Waites had quarterbacked earlier Bulldog expeditions, which couldn't get in. Now it was little Pete Allen's turn again. He sent Harbin for five yards on first down, but two more tries by the Bulldog left halfback showed a yard loss. On the second one, trying to pass, Harbin had been flattened, and time-out was called.

Charley Wilcox from Mobile was waved into the game as a substitute for Harbin, but Harrison, the captain, a man who seemed almost to swagger when he walked on a football field, wasn't having that. He refused to accept the substitute. Harbin stayed in for fourth down, and this one had to be a pass. Harbin went back, and he looked and he waited and he looked again. Then he threw. It wasn't such a pretty pass. It might have wobbled a little, but Snell had loped into the open at the goal with his peculiar ground-eating gait, and if Dan Snell could get to a football he could catch it. He stopped for a second as the ball finished its long journey. Then he took it, shook off a tackler, and stepped into the end zone with a touchdown.

Now it was up to Penrod, a chunky hard-as-nails guy with cold black hair beginning to fall back a bit from his forehead. Cooper went over the ball, put it to Allen good and true, and Allen set it down just so. Penny Penrod kicked better-looking extra points in his Howard time. This one just got over the crossbar, but that's as far as it wanted to go. The game was tied, and that's the way it would end, quite gloriously for Howard, which was down at the Alabama thirty-four yard line throwing for a winning touchdown when the gun ended this Crimson Tide unhappiness.

Someone said that Pat Harrison walked to the Alabama side of the field and asked Coach Thomas, "Am I still too little?" because fresh out of high school he had been rejected by the Tide, and Pat might have done it. Thomas still had a role to play in this drama. Bancroft and his Bulldogs were whooping it up in their dressing room when Alabama's coach came knocking on the door. He had the game ball in his hands. "It's yours," he said to the Howard squad. "You deserve it."

That night there was a parade in downtown Birmingham as Howard students whooped it up, and even the Alabama people said you couldn't blame them.

14

The Great Robbery

September 29, 1954

BASEBALL'S RECORD BOOKS ARE FULL OF Willie Mays, but record books are for cold figures, and the arithmetic of the business couldn't interest Willie less, because that's what happened yesterday and Willie Mays of Fairfield, Alabama, has spent his life being interested only in the game being played today, right now, this minute. Yesterday is gone, tomorrow is too far away. The present has always been quite enough for a man who was born to play ball.

Mays played it as a kid in Fairfield, and he played it with the Birmingham Black Barons in the time when the Negro American League was big business because the major leagues were for white men only. Willie played stickball in the streets of New York. Always he played, and it was with a joyousness infecting all who saw him until more recent years when, perhaps, the gradual fading of the great skill began to stir unhappiness in him, and that would not have been an unnatural reaction. I'm certain that the young Willie Mays must have thought that surely the wonderful picnic would go on forever, as it was in 1954.

The books, the histories, must make the statistical hero of the World Series of that year a journeyman ballplayer named Jim (Dusty) Rhodes from Montgomery, who decided three games for the New York Giants with his pinch-hitting and found himself catapulted into a limelight that had lost him a year or so later.

Dusty was for right then; Willie was for all time, and men who are not bound by the book, who saw it happen, knew that on the afternoon of September 29 in the old Polo Grounds where John McGraw, Christy Matthewson, Carl Hubbell, Mel Ott, and Bill Terry had played themselves into baseball history, Mays might have had the one most magnificent moment of his thoroughly magnificent career.

He didn't do it with his bat, either. Mays was 0 for 3 that day, though he had won the National League batting championship, coming out of the Army in the spring to lead the Giants to a four-straight conquest of favored Cleveland in the Series. Offensively, his only contribution was to draw a base on balls from Bob Lemon that preceded the tenth-inning pinch-hit home run by Rhodes down the foul line to the 270-foot right field corner that made a 5–2 win for New York in the first game.

This was a catch. Men who saw it happen would refer to it always as The Catch when they talked about the World Series of 1954. Without The Catch, there wouldn't have been a tenth inning for Leo Durocher to send Rhodes to the plate to pull his high pop out of the park. Dusty wouldn't have gotten there, and Cleveland would have won the first game, and then it would have been an entirely different batch of baseball.

Willie Mays was twenty-three years old and about as close to heaven as mortal man could get when he went long-striding to center field with his pants legs almost to his ankle tops, as he always wore them, for the start of the Series that late-September day in New York, with 52,751 wedged into the Polo Grounds.

The Indians jumped Sal Maglie, the old Barber, for two runs in the first inning, but the Giants got two back in the third off Lemon, and

Going . . . going . . . gone . . . in Willie Mays's glove! This was The Catch against Cleveland. (Courtesy Associated Press/Wide World Photos)

that's the way they went through the fourth, fifth, sixth, and seventh. Something had to give sometime, and in the eighth inning it appeared that something had.

Maglie walked Larry Doby. Al Rosen followed with a single, his only hit of the game, and Durocher sent in Don Liddle to pitch to Vic Wertz, the Cleveland slugger, who already was 4 for 4 for the day. In a moment, this looked like a Durocher mistake.

There was a pitch, and Wertz, the big left-handed slugger, went after it with every ounce of power in him. The ball was a missile orbiting, long and high and deep to left-center, into the deepest part of the Polo Grounds. Stunned Giants stood, transfixed, watching it fly, but Willie Mays was running. He was running like he'd never run in his life. Once he looked back, over his shoulder, never slowing, running for Leo, running for the Giants, running because he was Willie Mays.

"I knew it was going to be far out," he told the *Birmingham News*'s Alf Van Hoose after the game, talking it over with a writer who had known him when he was still at Birmingham, playing only the home games with the Black Barons because he was still in school at Fairfield Industrial High and too young to make the road trips.

Everybody in the ballpark knew it was far out.

"I thought it would stay in," Mays said.

His sure instincts told Mays correctly. He ran with his back to the diamond, on and on, and then, at the last possible instant, he turned again, threw up his hands, and Wertz's smash died there, taken over the shoulder of the Giants' centerfielder and turned into an out. Now Mays jammed on the brakes, whirled, and almost in one motion, with his cap flying off, lined his throw back to the infield. Doby, near third base, watching, scurried back to first. These were two runs the Indians never got, because Marv Grissom replaced Liddle, walked one, struck out one, and Jim Hegan, the catcher, lifted an easy fly to Monte Irvin.

Cleveland hung on for a while, but Cleveland was doomed, and The Catch had done it, the impossible, spectacular, wonderful robbery that only Mays, the incomparable, could have pulled off.

One was out in the tenth when Mays worked Lemon for a walk on five pitches. Henry Thompson was up, and Durocher had him taking as Mays took off for second, and he was there—minus cap—ahead of the throw. Now, Thompson was walked intentionally, and here came Dusty Rhodes. Three seconds later, and Willie Mays was jumping up and down out between second and third in wild, unbridled happiness, because Rhodes had found his home-run pitch, had uppercutted it, high and hugging the foul line, into the seats in right. A teammate finally grabbed Mays and shoved him on his way so that the winning procession could come around behind him.

Rhodes went on to get four big hits in the Series, two home runs and two singles, driving in seven runs, but the Giants didn't need him, even on the last day. Cleveland had caved in, and lost 7–4, and it was one for the books. Rhodes was telling the writers, "I just love to hit," and professing to some anger at Durocher for not starting him in a game, but the Series had been perfect for him, one moment of grandeur in a lifetime of baseball.

New York sports columnist Jimmy Cannon wrote, "The Indians didn't quit or they didn't choke. They just didn't become involved. . . . The losers' share depresses most teams, but the Indians won it justly."

The Catch had greased the skids to Cleveland disaster. One second, the Indians—who had won 111 games in an American League runaway—had it in their hands, and maybe they could have won with that impetus. Another second and they were stone-cold dead and Willie Mays was stopping, turning, throwing while his cap flew away. This was the best beginning to be for the boy from Fairfield. You can't read it in the record books. They won't have a line about The Catch.

There is another story, too, that must not be lost; and that one was told me on a hot summer afternoon in Birmingham in July of 1965. It was the day after Mays had hit his 471st home run on the way to becoming the National League's all-time home-run king. Bill Maughn, a scout who would die later that summer, told it to me.

Maughn, who scouted then for the Boston Braves, was the man who found Willie Mays and never got to sign him. Maughn was the guy who struck it richest on the Klondike and didn't get to file the claim; he found the pot of gold at the end of the rainbow and they wouldn't let him pick it up; he slew the dragon to win the hand of the princess fair and found out she had run off with the king's boy next door.

Bill Maughn had pennants in his hand, in bunches like bananas, thrusting them at the Boston Braves who would become Milwaukee's, and then Atlanta's.

"I had been to Tuscaloosa," Maughn said, "and this would have been, let me see, 1949. I stopped by Rickwood and the Black Barons were playing Dallas. I just walked in with no lineups, not expecting anything, really.

"The left fielder for Birmingham couldn't throw. Dallas had runners on first and third and it was in the second inning. The next hitter hit the ball off the scoreboard, and the left fielder got it. The center fielder came running over yelling, 'Give it to me, give it to me!' And be-doggoned if the left fielder didn't shovel-pass it to him like a football player and the center fielder threw out the runner trying to go from first to third.

"Four innings later, he goes to right-center and he has to turn and throw and he gets another one by eight feet, trying to go from first to third.

"I didn't know anyone there, but I looked up the owner, Tom Hayes. He told me the center fielder's name. It was Willie Mays, and he would be eligible to sign next year when he got out of high school.

"I followed him for sixteen games the rest of that year and the spring of the next, and all he ever thought about or talked about was playing ball. He was pleading with me to sign him by then, but the Braves had just paid $150,000 for Sam Jethroe, their first black player, and they moved slower back then, as you know. They weren't sure about Willie, so they sent a liaison man down from the front office to look at him. He saw Willie once, and it was a doubleheader and Willie was up eight times and didn't get a hit. He said he couldn't stay any longer to see him again. He had to go to Texas, so forget about it.

"A few weeks later, I was in Atlanta and tipped off Eddie Montague, who scouted for the Giants. Eddie was coming to Birmingham to look at Alonzo Perry, who played first base for the Black Barons. 'Listen,' I told him, 'you forget about Perry. Willie Mays is the one you want.' So Montague and another Giant scout, Bill Harris, came to Birmingham and they saw Willie and decided to take him. They didn't have to wait.

"He cost them $14,000. They gave Tom Hayes, the owner, $10,000 and Willie $4,000. I could have signed him for $6,000. 'Mr. Maughn,' he'd say, 'why don't you go ahead and sign me?' and I'd have to say, 'Not yet.'

"He went to Trenton that first year and he was at Minneapolis for a while in 1961, then they took him up. He was 0 for 26 at the start, but Durocher stuck with him and played him, and the rest is in the book.

"Do you think he'd have made a difference for the Braves when they lost the pennant by one game in 1956, or in 1959, when they tied? What an outfield they'd have had," Maughn sighed, "with Henry Aaron (another great Alabama big leaguer, from Mobile) and Mays still in the same outfield. That guy the Braves sent down—I can't remember his name—must have made one of the most expensive trips to Texas any representative of any baseball team ever had. The Giants got Willie for $14,000 and he made millions for them, and all the Braves had to say was, 'Come on.' I wish they had said it," said the man who had the key to Fort Knox and found that someone had changed the lock.

Maughn's assumption, of course, was that Mays's great gifts would have done it for anyone like they've done it for the Giants, in New York, then in San Francisco. Probably yes, but possibly no. This much is certain: if the Braves had listened in 1949 to a scout in the Deep South, Willie Mays wouldn't have been at the Polo Grounds on September 29, 1954, to make The Catch that slammed the door on the Cleveland Indians and opened it wide, for a little while, for a pinch hitter named Dusty Rhodes, who sat on the bench while Mays ran toward baseball immortality.

15

A Day for Believers

January 1, 1966

THE THINGS THAT TOOK PLACE ON January 1, 1966, in college football would have been far too improbable ever to have sold to the movies, even back in the days when all of them ended with hero and heroine in a happy clinch because everything had worked out just right, the mortgage on the ranch had been paid off, the poor boy had become president of the firm or some such.

On the night of January 1, 1966, in the Orange Bowl, Alabama won its third national football championship in five years.

On the morning of January 1, 1966, Alabama ranked no better than No. 3 because during the regular run of 1965 Alabama had lost to Georgia in the last minute and had been tied by Tennessee. Michigan State was No. 1 and Arkansas was No. 2, but the final vote in the Associated Press rankings—granddaddy of them all—waited until the conclusion of the bowl games because of the involvement of these three—the Spartans, the Razorbacks, the Crimson Tide.

Michigan State would finish up against UCLA in the Rose Bowl, and Michigan State was favored.

Arkansas had Louisiana State in the Cotton Bowl. Arkansas was supposed to win.

Alabama had made it to the Orange Bowl with a strong stretch run, there to meet a Nebraska team that outweighed Tidesmen thirty-five pounds to the man.

Paul Bryant, the coach, talked hopefully in private to his players about what could happen. They still had a shot at the big prize, he insisted, and they believed, because Bryant inspires this kind of confidence in young men. But even Bryant must have known that the odds against this Alabama team's winding up with a second straight national championship were only slightly less than astronomical.

First, Arkansas, champion of the Southwest Conference, must lose to a Louisiana State team that had been thrashed 31–7 by Alabama back in November.

Then, one of Duffy Daugherty's mightiest Michigan State teams from the Big Ten must fall to Tommy Prothro's Uclans, and certainly the Coast team didn't belong on the same field, even if more than 100,000 were coming to see them play.

And, if Arkansas should lose in the early afternoon and Michigan State should lose in the later afternoon, Alabama had to win in the balmy Miami night from a powerhouse Nebraska which many thought had the strength to pitch the Tide out into Biscayne Bay.

This stage hadn't been set properly at all, not for the hopes of Alabamians who had cheered national champs in 1961 and 1964 put together by Bryant.

"We have one chance of winning this football game," a grim Bryant told writers close to him like the *Birmingham News*'s Alf Van Hoose and Tuscaloosa's Charley Land two days before kickoff.

"Our only chance is to keep the football. I've told Steve (Sloan, the quarterback) to come out throwing and to keep on throwing, and (this in violation of every Bryant tenet) I don't care if we're backed up to the one-yard line. We're going to throw the ball anywhere and I mean it. They could run us out of the stadium if we don't keep the ball."

This, then, was the plan to which Alabama was committed as the

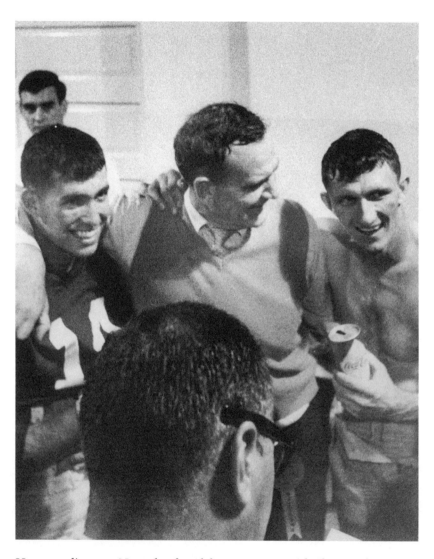

Happy ending to a No. 1 day for Alabama: Bryant with Sloan and
Perkins. (Courtesy *Birmingham News*)

sun burst out over Miami on Saturday, January 1. The players slept late, before the night game, to which the Orange Bowl had committed itself the year before when Texas won from Alabama and the television ratings spiraled up, and so did the price of future contracts. In the early afternoon they could see for themselves the beginning of the fairy-tale ending now developing.

The first chapter was at Dallas in the Cotton Bowl. Charlie McClendon, who had played for Bryant at Kentucky and coached for him, and his Louisiana State Tigers were ready. They clamped Arkansas's Razorbacks in the kind of defensive vise that characterizes McClendon teams. They won 10–7.

The second chapter was kicking off at Pasadena in the Rose Bowl, famous old steel-and-concrete structure, king of them all, a mammoth place but dwarfed by the mountains that seem close enough to touch, high enough to be crowned by snow, dimly white in the distance. They fought it out, the home boys from UCLA and the champs of the Big Ten, and this was UCLA's prize.

The crowd was filing into the Orange Bowl when the final returns came in from out west, 14–12, for UCLA, and here you are, Alabama; or, maybe Nebraska, which was No. 4 on the national list.

Sloan, the deeply devout young man from Cleveland, Tennessee, who had been converted during the season into a backup passer after two years as a quarterback who'd roll out mostly, to run or to throw, tipped Alabama's hand right away. The first time the Tide got the football, on its thirty-nine, in the first quarter, Steve put the Bryant Plan into operation. He passed.

The first pitch was a seven-yarder to tackle Jerry Duncan on the Alabama tackle-eligible maneuver whose success finally would have college rules-makers shooting at it. It took eight plays, Sloan passing, Les Kelley and Steve Bowman running, to send the Tide into a 7–0 lead. The touchdown was a twenty-one-yard pass to Ray Perkins, and David Ray kicked the point.

Late in the first quarter, Ray missed a nineteen-yard field goal attempt, and Nebraska struck back early in the second to tie the score. The touchdown was a thirty-four-yard pass to Tony Jeter. Larry Wachholtz kicked. Alabama's defense was about to be penetrated for more points than a Bryant-coached team ever had allowed. No one on the Alabama side would complain about this afterward, however. Not in the least.

Alabama struck back, going seventy yards on nine plays, after a roughing-the-kicker penalty provided new life. The big gainer was a thirty-nine-yard pass from Sloan to Perkins, and the catch was a diving spectacular. This put the ball on the twelve. Bowman took care of eight, and after Kelley stormed in, Ray made it 14–7.

The next time Alabama got the football was back on its seven-yard line. What to do from there with a seven-point lead and halftime getting close? Play it safe? Not this night. Sloan passed, right off, twenty-seven yards to Perkins, and the express was rolling again. Dennis Homan caught a pass, Wayne Cook another, and there was an interference call on the Nebraska eleven, followed by another Sloan pass to Perkins for a touchdown. Ray made it 21–7 with 1:42 remaining before intermission.

Alabama insisted on keeping the football. Vernon Newbill recovered the onside kick that followed, and Sloan fired thirty-six yards to Perkins forthwith. On fourth down, with time fleeting, Ray kicked a nineteen-yard field goal. When the teams went to rest, Alabama led 24–7 and would not be in real danger again.

Nebraska pulled closer in the third quarter with a forty-nine-yard pass from Bob Churchich to Ben Gregory, with Gregory in the clear and all alone for the last twenty-five yards. A pass for a two-pointer failed, and Alabama, which had opened up Nebraska defenses with its wide-open first-half passing, now capitalized on the ground. The Tide swept sixty-nine yards, every inch of it on the ground, with the longest gain a nine-yard run by Kelley. Frank Canterbury set up the score with a seven-yarder to the one. Bowman scored, and just to demonstrate, possibly, that the air had not been forsaken, Sloan passed to Perkins for a two-point conversion.

They went into the fourth quarter with Alabama on top 32–13. Nebraska made a touchdown, driving fifty-five yards with Churchich sneaking the last one, and Wachholtz kicked point.

Alabama made a touchdown right back, going fifty-five also, with Bowman taking the last two and Ray converting. Bryant was clearing the bench now, letting everyone have fun, and Nebraska wouldn't play dead. The Cornhuskers revved up for a final touchdown on a Jeter catch of a fourteen-yard Churchich pass, followed by a two-point conversion.

All of this added up to 39–28 for Bryant's lightweights. Sloan set a record with twenty pass completions in twenty-nine attempts. "The most accurate passer" Bryant had ever coached gained 296 yards with them, and Perkins's ten catches were an Orange Bowl record too. Kelley gained 116 of Alabama's 222 yards running behind the blocks of Cecil Dowdey, Paul Crane, and John Calvert.

"I've never been in a game like this before," Alabama's coach was heard saying in the wildly happy dressing room.

No one there had seen one like it either; nor had the Associated Press voters among the millions watching on television across the nation.

In another week, they voted, and no one really had doubted the outcome of the election.

Alabama was No. 1 again because everything that had to happen did happen. If Hollywood had had it in the old days, there would have been the hero and the heroine and you know the rest. But not even Hollywood would have taken that day and that story and tried to make it sound real. It just didn't add up, but shortly after this the first of the signs appeared that would adorn the automobiles of Bryant-admirers.

They read, "I believe."

16

Grand Champion

July 25, 1953

TWELVE OF THEM CAME, CRACKING jokes about their eyes that couldn't see, to the National Blind Golf championship in July of 1953 at Highland Park in Birmingham. Twelve brave men who walked in a world eternally dark and laughed at it, and Charley Boswell, the defending champion, was one of them.

What's the difference if a man laughs sometimes to keep from crying? The wonderful thing is that he can laugh, and Boswell might have laughed louder and longer than any who had come to his hometown where for the first time all of his family could see him triumph. Family meaning his wife, Kitty, and the children, his mother and dad, his brothers and sisters and their wives and husbands, and nieces and nephews. The Boswell clan of Birmingham is large. It's also close.

Charley Boswell had arrived at this amazing golf tournament, played by blind men, from a time when he had no laugh in him at all, and in that time was the beginning of this story. . . .

It was November 30, 1944, near the little town of Lindern in the Ruhr Valley. Captain Charles Boswell, infantry company commander, was riding back to his company in a tank after a hurry-up trip for supplies to fight Germans off of Lindern.

The trip was almost done when a German shell exploded into the tank, and now it had become a sitting duck. The men inside scrambled out and into a ditch for safety.

Captain Boswell was headed out when he looked back and saw the gunner, just a boy, stunned and still in the tank. He went back, forced the limp figure out the open hatch over to the ground. At this instant, the next shot hit. It was about four o'clock in the afternoon.

Seven days later, his eyes covered by bandages, Captain Boswell awoke in an Army hospital. Medics picking up American dead the next day had come upon him beside the shattered tank and found a spark of life in the twenty-seven-year-old who had been hit in the chest and head.

Then the long journey began, one hospital to another, one operation after another on the eyes. Belgium, England, Wales, and finally in March of 1945 Boswell was back in this country, and the military hospital at Valley Forge, Pennsylvania, had him.

All the long way, Boswell had hoped that somehow, someway he would see again. Occasionally a doctor would offer some small encouragement, though never very much. On his second day at Valley Forge, the day his pretty young wife would arrive to see the soldier gone so long, Charley Boswell found out.

Dr. Elliott Randolph, who would go on to become one of the nation's eminent eye surgeons, was as new at Valley Forge as his patient. There were all the checks to do again, the examinations, and, at last, the doctor was delivering the message he didn't want to deliver.

"Boz, old boy," he said, "Everything has been done, but ... " He went on to tell how much a man could do who had lost his vision. Charley Boswell didn't hear him. He asked the orderly to take him back to his room. By himself, he cried.

Now the blinded infantryman himself had a message to deliver. His wife was there, and he couldn't make himself tell her. They had a room at a small hotel downtown for their reunion, and the next night had come. They sat together and tried to make conversation, and Kitty Boswell knew that not all of the story had been told yet.

She walked across the room and looked down on the head of the man who had been an outstanding University of Alabama halfback and professional baseball prospect before he left for war. He felt her close, and suddenly she was seated in his lap and her arms were around him.

"You tell me," she said. "You tell me all of it. Nothing is going to make any difference with us."

So he told her. They cried together. Their tears were for each other.

A man like Boswell doesn't run from trouble, not when he has a Kitty Boswell.

There was a rehabilitation program at Valley Forge for soldiers who were blinded during the war. Captain Boswell tried everything, but bowling, riding, swimming held no answers for him. Would anything?

Maybe a month after Charley Boswell knew that he could never see again, Corporal Kenny Gleason, who worked in Valley Forge rehabilitation, showed up with something new. "Captain," the corporal said, "let's go play some golf."

The captain's reaction was that he was in no frame of mind for jokes and maybe the corporal had better get out before he threw him out, but the corporal persisted.

Almost, he convinced Boswell that he could teach him, a blind man, to play golf, and they went to a golf course nearby to try. Boswell insisted that Gleason get him off out of the way, out of view, for he didn't want to be seen occupied with this business by people who could see.

Gleason handed him a two wood, showed a man who had never played golf how the club should be held, had him practice-swing a time or two.

Then Gleason teed up a ball, got his patient in place beside it, brought the club head down for him addressing the ball, then said, "Swing at it."

Charley Boswell plants his feet and swings away—in golf, in life.
(Courtesy *Birmingham News*)

Boswell swung.

Hit a golf ball once right on the nose, and you'll know the feeling. Charley Boswell knew that he'd caught that one on the screws, busted it good. Gleason told him that he had gone two hundred yards straight. If he could hit one, he could hit another. And another and another, and then they played two holes, and Boswell knew he had found something that was for him.

Soon he was out for eighteen holes and scoring no more than 120 with Gleason lining up shots, describing the layout, lining up putts, and they played through the spring and the summer of 1945, Boswell getting better and better, enjoying himself more and more. Here was solid accomplishment. His mastery of a game might have set a pattern for the later years when he would become a well-to-do Birmingham citizen in the insurance business. At the moment, the game was sufficient unto itself.

In the spring of 1946, Charley Boswell came home to Birmingham to stay. One of the first calls he made was to an old friend, Grant Thomas, newly out of the Navy. "Hey, Grant," Boswell told him on the telephone, "let's go play some golf."

Thomas said, "How in the world do you think *you* could play golf?"

Then they went out, and Boswell showed Thomas how it was he could play golf.

In December of 1946, financed by a friend at Loveman's department store in Birmingham where he sold sporting goods, Boswell went to his first tournament at Los Angeles, and Thomas went as his "coach," the man who would be his eyes on the golf course for many years along with Bill Mogge and Bo Russell, close friends, too, and cousin Dick Cox.

Boswell didn't win the first tournament, though he got to play golf with Bob Hope and Bing Crosby, and Hope, particularly, became a friend for life. In 1947 at Duluth, the champion was Charley Boswell of Birmingham, and he had won four in a row when the tournament was scheduled for Highland Park—later renamed Charley Boswell—a hilly municipal course on Birmingham's Southside.

The format was thirty-six holes—eighteen on Saturday, eighteen on Sunday—at medal play, and pre-tournament conversation from the contestants for the newspapers was typical. Bob Allman of Philadelphia came to town with this: "I think Charley ought to be examined before we start playing Saturday. I'm not sure he's blind. He plays golf too well. He must peep."

There was a unique putting contest the day before to settle a three-way tie in the Scotch foursome the blind golfers had played with professional partners. The pros were blindfolded and putted from about forty feet on the ninth hole. One of them five-putted, another four-putted and didn't get in the hole. The winner, S. A. Smith, took first by getting closest. Afterward he said, "I didn't have any idea how hard to hit the ball, or on what line. The putter felt like it weighed twice as much as it does when I can see what I'm doing." They had a small idea of what handicaps the tournament contestants had overcome to play.

There was a feeling that Boswell, on a course he knew best, might run away with it, but the championship he sought before home folks didn't come that easily. After Saturday's opening eighteen holes, Boswell's balky putter left him in second place at 106. The leader was Joe Lazaro, a sweet swinger from Waltham, Massachusetts, who had lost his sight when a mine exploded beneath him during World War II in Italy. Lazaro led the way into the final round with a smooth 103 over the par-70 Highland layout, a fairly short course, but full of trouble for any man who strayed from its hills.

July 26 in Birmingham can be steaming hot. This July 26, the second and last day of the tournament, was all of that and more. Boswell and Lazaro were playing together before a gallery that numbered more than four thousand, and Charley wanted the victory as much, almost, as he had ever wanted anything in his life.

It was the sort of pressurized situation that brings out the best in an athlete like Boswell. The adrenaline surges. Just about all of those people ready to walk up and down Highland's slopes had come to see a man play golf—and win—whom they had only read about before.

So Boswell nailed his drive on No. 1 just as he had that first time when he was finding his way from hopelessness at Valley Forge in the spring of 1945. Hit it like the first time. Hit it better.

The tee shot was 230 yards, straight away. Lazaro, attempting to match it, hooked into the rough and couldn't get out of trouble. Boswell was on in three, down in two putts for a five. Lazaro had ten, and the champion from Birmingham was on the way. Boswell had 51 going out, 584 776 554.

It was 55 coming in, due to a ten on No. 11 where one out-of-bounds shot and another in a lake got in the way, but Boswell had it in his pocket by now. His second straight 106 was good for 212, and that made him the winner by ten strokes over Peter Bell of Detroit, who slipped past the unlucky Lazaro to a second-place 222 off 133 and 109. Lazaro was third with 224.

Boswell would win many more tournaments (he had fifteen national championships and eleven in international play) as this record was set down in the spring of 1968, but none of them had what the 1953 victory had. This one was at home.

There was a cheer to split the sky when Boswell ran his last putt down for a six on No. 18, and someone was rushing to shake hands and pat him on the back. Somewhere in that mob was his family, or most of his family. One member had deserted the pack. There was commotion as a seven-year-old carbon copy of the national blind golf champion came scrambling through the people who wouldn't let his father free, and then Charles Boswell Jr. had thrown himself into his father's arms and wrapped his legs around him to let the whole world know that this man belonged to him.

Later, Chuck Boswell's weary father said, "This was the big one. This was the tournament I wanted most to win. My feet ache, my bones ache, my whole body aches, but I feel like a million."

So did all the other Boswells—mother, father, sisters, brothers, nieces, nephews, and the girl who had cried with him one night at Valley Forge, Pennsylvania, surely a century ago when she said, "It doesn't matter," and somehow they made it be true.

Charley Boswell may be Alabama's greatest sports story, though he never shot a 70 in his game in his life, never saw the heart-bursting beauty of a golf course stretched out before him early in the morning, demanding a challenge. Major Charles A. Boswell, U.S. Infantry (Ret.), is a lesson in limitless courage and undaunted human spirit that goes far beyond games. You hear it, you know it when he laughs, and the laugh is that of a brave, free man.

17

A Father-Son Day at Daytona

CLYDE BOLTON

MOST FATHERS WANT THEIR SONS to get ahead, but on February 15, 1988, that was the last thing Bobby Allison wished for his son Davey.

That's because they were stock car drivers, two stars of NASCAR's elite Winston Cup circuit, and they found themselves running 1-2 in the Super Bowl of the sport, the Daytona 500.

Bobby got his wish. The fifty-year-old Hueytown, Alabama, resident edged his twenty-year-old neighbor by two and a half car lengths at Daytona International Speedway.

In the post-race press conference, Bobby didn't have to ponder to name his biggest day in racing. "You'd sure have to say this was it," he told reporters.

It was a dream come true for Davey—almost. "I've dreamed about this for years," he said. "Since I was a kid, I've dreamed about a down-to-the-wire battle with Dad. But in my dreams I won."

One of the greatest stories in Alabama sports history was written that day in Florida. Coincidentally, the setting of the stage had begun many years before in the Sunshine State.

Bobby Allison had grown up in the Miami area, and one day when he was nine years old he attended a stock car race with his grandfather. The sounds and smells, the thrill of the chase reverberated in his mind, and he could barely sleep that night. He became an inveterate drawer of race cars on the pages of his school notebook. He believes his future was decided by that trip to a speedway.

He went out for football in high school, but his coach pictured all sorts of disasters involving a 110-pound boy playing with others who weighed twice as much. The coach urged him to try other extracurricular activities.

So, whatever glory Bobby would find in sports would have to wait. Instead of becoming a football player, he became the manager of the football, basketball, baseball, and track teams.

People with a talent for gardening are said to have green thumbs. Bobby must have had a black thumb, for he had a talent for repairing anything broken. He worked on his priest's car. He traded a motorcycle for a 1938 Chevrolet and babied it as if it were, well, a child. It would become his first race car.

Bobby was one of thirteen children born to Ed and Katherine Allison. He was fifth in line, and sixth was his brother Donnie. Who would have guessed they would change the face of automobile racing in Alabama?

Bobby set his course to drive race cars after that visit to a track with his grandfather, but Donnie could have found his niche in diving or in one-horsepower racing.

Donnie won the Florida state AAU diving championship, and he was offered a college scholarship if he would attend a certain high school. But it was a public school, and he wanted to attend a Catholic school.

A horse trainer met him at a swimming pool. The trainer was impressed by his lack of size and his competitive nature. Under the trainer's influence, Donnie decided to become a jockey. Donnie began working as an exercise-boy apprentice at Tropical Park.

He was sixteen years old and riding his motorcycle on the way to feed a horse when the course of his life changed. A truck stopped in front of him, and there was a crash. His left leg was mangled.

Donnie was left with a limp and one leg shorter than the other. He was hospitalized thirteen weeks. When he entered the hospital he weighed 100 pounds; when he was dismissed he weighed 125. It was the beginning of a growth spurt and the end of his aspirations to be a jockey.

Hialeah Speedway created an amateur division in 1955, and Bobby Allison saw an opportunity to race. He drove the 1938 Chevrolet, the same car that took him to school, and finished seventh in a forty-car field. The next week he was seventh again; the third week he scored his first victory as a race driver.

After high school Bobby worked for Carl Kiekhaefer's powerhouse racing team, which fielded cars for such stars as Buck Baker, Tim Flock, and Herb Thomas. He turned wrenches at the Charlotte shop and learned the value of organization and preventive maintenance. He learned that racing is not only a sport but also a business.

Bobby returned to Miami and worked for a noted driver of that area, Red Farmer. In later years Farmer would be Donnie Allison's crew chief. Bobby also resumed his driving career.

The Florida short tracks paid poor purses, but Bobby heard about a land of milk and honey for bullring racers—Alabama—so he and brother Donnie boarded a pickup truck and towed his race car to the Heart of Dixie. It was 1959. They slept in the truck. They bought a basket of peaches for fifty cents and had peaches for breakfast, lunch, and supper.

It was during their second week in Alabama that Bobby scored his first professional victory, at Montgomery. That same night Donnie drove in his first race after another Florida driver decided to go home and the car's owner let the younger Allison drive the car.

They returned to Florida, and Bobby told Red Farmer: "Red, Alabama is beautiful, the race tracks are great, and the people are the nicest you ever met. You need to go to Alabama with us."

The Allisons and Farmer made the trek to Alabama time and time again, frequently outrunning the disgruntled locals, who called them "gypsies."

Eventually they moved to the Birmingham area, settling in Hueytown, which now was on its way to becoming the biggest little town in stock car racing. From their Hueytown base they traveled together to other states, and they frequently ran 1-2-3. "Oh, no, there's that Alabama gang," a disappointed driver at a North Carolina track said as they towed their race cars through the pit gate. A nickname was born. They became the Alabama Gang, a designation that would later include Davey Allison and Hueytown neighbor Neil Bonnett and, when used loosely, every Alabama driver.

The Allison brothers graduated from the short tracks to the Winston Cup circuit. Donnie would win ten Cup races. Bobby's eighty-four victories during a big-league career that stretched from 1965 into 1988 tied him for third on the all-time list.

The 1983 season was especially noteworthy for the Allison family. Bobby had been runner-up for the Winston Cup championship five times—in 1970, 1972, 1978, 1981, and 1982. Was he to be the most famous bridesmaid in the sport's history? Nope. He won the title in 1983 to escape that distinction. He also won the American Driver of the Year award, racing's equivalent of football's Heisman Trophy. Also in 1983, on April 30, Davey Allison scored the first superspeedway victory of his career. It came in a 500-kilometer ARCA race at Talladega.

Davey had been born in Florida, but he grew up in Hueytown. He entered the world on February 25, 1961. That was the day before the Daytona 500, and the day after his father had competed in his first Winston Cup race, a Daytona 500 qualifier.

Soon after the finish of the qualifying event, Bobby was told to rush home. He jumped into a pickup truck and sped to the hospital in

Hollywood, Florida, where his wife, Judy, gave birth to a boy. Bobby stayed with them as long as he could and then rushed back to Daytona Beach, where he finished thirty-first in the 500 on February 26.

Davey, of course, grew up in a racing atmosphere, one he found fascinating.

"Davey was always a competitor," remembered Red Farmer. "He and Clifford used to come into the shop on tricycles racing each other. We'd be there working in race cars, and we'd have to run them out. . . .

"A few years later they'd come racing through there on bicycles."

Clifford Allison was Davey's brother. He lost his life in a racing-practice crash in Michigan in 1992.

Davey swept and did other chores in his father's racing shop. He and some friends built a limited sportsman racer, and he made his racing debut on April 22, 1979, finishing fifth in the feature at Birmingham.

Like his father, Davey worked his way up the racing ladder. He won on the short tracks, became ARCA's all-time superspeedway winner, and in 1987 became Winston Cup Rookie of the Year. He won a pair of races that year and became the first rookie ever to win twice. His first victory came at the Winston 500 at Talladega on May 3 in just his fourteenth Cup start. Two races later he won the Budweiser 500 at Dover.

Bobby figured prominently in that Winston 500. His car became airborne after a tire blowout and wiped out thirty-five yards of the frontstretch catch fence before falling back onto the racing surface. The race was red-flagged for two hours, thirty-eight minutes, and fourteen seconds while the fence was repaired. The incident led to the infamous carburetor restrictor plates that are still used to slow the cars.

Those two worthies, father and son, squared off in the 1988 Daytona 500, and their 1-2 finish made it one of the most memorable events in stock car racing history.

Bobby signaled that he was in for a special Speed Weeks at Daytona

In 1981 Bobby Allison and son Davey shared this light moment. Less than seven years later they roared to a dramatic 1-2 finish in the Daytona 500. (Courtesy *Birmingham News*)

by winning one of Thursday's twin 125-mile qualifying races and by taking Saturday's Goody's 300 sportsman event. Now with fifteen victories, he was tied with Cale Yarborough as the speedway's most successful driver. He had a chance to break the deadlock in Sunday's Daytona 500.

Every time fifty-year-old Bobby Allison won a Winston Cup race, he extended his record as the oldest man to do so. After his victory in the qualifying race, he fielded the usual questions as to whether his age affected his racing. "The only problem I have," he said, "is getting up early on a day when I don't have a race to go to."

The preliminaries weren't so good to Davey. In the final practice on Saturday, his car scraped the wall and his crew spent hours making the repairs. After he ran second to his father in the Daytona 500 he said, "I would like to have seen how things would have turned out if we hadn't had that crash yesterday."

He wasn't using his incident as an excuse, but he had to wonder what would have happened if his car hadn't been pounded and perhaps knocked a tad off max.

The thirtieth Daytona 500 was one for the books. A crowd of 135,000 saw Bobby's Buick edge Davey's Ford by two and a half car lengths.

Davey faked to the outside and tried to pull to the inside coming out of the fourth turn of the last lap, but he didn't have the horsepower to seriously challenge Pop.

"My only hope was to get alongside and beat him by two inches because I don't think I could have ever gotten all the way around him," Davey said. "I couldn't do it."

"I saw the nose of his car out of the corner of my eye," Bobby said, "but I really thought I had enough suds to beat him."

Davey said he gave it all he had and wasn't content with being runner-up in the biggest stock car event. "I definitely didn't settle for second place anytime in this race," he said, "and I never felt I didn't have a chance to win it or that my chances were slim."

It was the first 1-2 finish involving a father and son in Winston Cup racing since Lee Petty beat his son Richard on a short track in Pittsburgh in 1960. Lee had beaten Richard at Lakewood Speedway in Atlanta in 1959 in the only other one.

Bobby Allison led seventy laps, more than anyone else, and Darrell Waltrip led sixty-nine. Davey Allison led only two, but he and his father and Waltrip had the three strongest racers. They had appeared headed for a three-car shootout before Waltrip's Chevrolet began slowing fifteen laps from the end. He held on for an eleventh-place finish.

"This is the best car I've ever had anywhere in my whole life, bar none," Waltrip said. "There at the end something internally in the motor gave out. I heard a noise and we started heading toward the back.

"It was really tough those last laps watching people I'd beaten all day pass me. Davey and Bobby just had it going their way, but I still think I could have beaten them if I hadn't had that last problem."

Phil Parsons finished third, and another Hueytown driver, Neil Bonnett, ran fourth in the lead draft. "If Neil had been third, they would have burned down Hueytown tonight," said Red Farmer, who was crew chief on Davey's sportsman car.

Bobby was delighted that his sixteenth victory made him the speedway's winningest driver. "That makes me feel real good," he said. "I didn't win a major event until late in my career, and that makes it especially nice."

The victory by a fifty-year-old athlete in his sport's premier event captured the imagination of the nation. Fifty-year-old golfers go to the Senior PGA Tour, but Bobby hung in there with the elite.

"I think it's directly related to the individual," he reflected after winning the Daytona 500. "One driver might be past his prime at forty, and another driver might go on. An example is Red Farmer, who gave a stirring performance in the ARCA race last Sunday.

"You find some individuals who are able to keep a handle on it, but it seems to slip away from others."

Watching that Daytona 500 was Judy Allison—Bobby's wife and Davey's mother. Asked if she had a favorite as the race sifted down to her husband and her son, she answered, "I was pulling for Bobby."

Why?

"I knew him first."

She smiled and added, "And he still pays the bills."

Judy called it her biggest day in racing. What better Valentine's Day present than seeing your husband earn $202,940 and your son $113,760?

"It's got to be neat for both of them," she said. "You think about a finish like that happening someday, but when it really happens you don't believe it."

Judy added, "I was biting my nails without biting my nails. I was hoping nothing would happen. I've seen so much happen on that last lap."

Daytona 500 finishes can get nasty, but neither driver considered the possibility this time.

"I've seen over the years how fair he is," Davey said. "I knew if I had the car to beat him, I'd beat him, and he wouldn't do anything out of the way."

"I've always played it straight," Bobby said, "and when I'm racing against the best youngster to come along I wouldn't do anything different."

On that happy day, who could have dreamed what was ahead for the winner and runner-up of the Daytona 500?

Four months later, on June 19, 1988, Bobby Allison was grievously injured in a crash at Pocono Raceway in Pennsylvania. It ended his racing career and necessitated a long period of recuperation. His injuries left blanks in his memory, and indeed, he doesn't remember edging his son in the Daytona 500.

On July 12, 1993, Davey Allison, who had nineteen Winston Cup victories to his credit and seemingly many more ahead of him, was fatally injured in a helicopter crash at Talladega Superspeedway.

18

An Open Gate for Jerry Pate

JIM MARTIN

IN A LETTER TO THE United States Golf Association, delivered only a few months before his death, Bobby Jones requested that the U.S. Open Championship be played at his home club, the Atlanta Athletic Club in Duluth, twenty-eight miles from downtown Atlanta.

That was not the site where Jones had grown up and learned the game. That was at old East Lake, not far from downtown. The membership decided to relocate in the early 1970s. Jones died in 1971, and the championship was awarded for 1976.

That was historic for a number of reasons. It was the first time the Open had been played in the Deep South. The Open is always played in June, and the USGA has always opted for moderate climate.

But this was Bob Jones's signature on the letter, and another southerner would assume the mantle Jones had won years before. His name was Jerry Pate, the 1974 U.S. Amateur champion, a title he had claimed while a junior at the University of Alabama.

Jones had been a four-time Open champion, of course, and a five-time Amateur champion.

Pate, in this memorable week, would join an exclusive list of men who had claim to both titles—Francis Ouimet, Gene Littler, Arnold Palmer, Jack Nicklaus, Lawson Little, and Jones.

Pate was twenty-two years old, making his first professional win in a major championship. A guy named Nicklaus had done that in 1962 in an Open playoff with Palmer at Oakmont.

Jerry Pate was born in Macon, Georgia, the family later moving to Anniston for eleven years before business took his father, Pat Pate, to Pensacola.

"I had three states pulling for me today," said Pate after his victory. "And I could hear 'em all."

Pate's father was a Coca-Cola executive in Pensacola and was associated with Crawford Rainwater Jr., whose father played many rounds with Jones and was instrumental in the founding of Augusta National Golf Club with Jones and Clifford Roberts.

The 1976 Open was a tribute to Jones.

"It's kind of funny," said the new champion, "with my background and all."

Another Jones connection was the tournament chairman, Eugene Branch, an Atlanta Athletic Club member and a law partner of Jones's. "After four days I would say this course has chosen its own," said Branch at the presentation ceremony. "And if Bob Jones were here today, I think he would say the course has chosen wisely."

The tournament site was a mix of some of the holes on the thirty-six-hole complex, most of which were adapted from the Highlands course. It started with wide-open but crunching par fours of 455, 450, and 460 yards. What would become the tournament back nine was more wooded with strategic water hazards as a chaser, particularly one that would figure in the final results, on the eighteenth.

The name of the tournament favorite was no surprise. In those days it was always Jack Nicklaus.

There was pre-tournament mention of others, such as:

Hale Irwin, the fiercely competitive man who always played well on the most difficult of courses, of which this was certainly one.

Jerry Pate, former University of Alabama golfer, is
pleased with his drive. (Courtesy U.S. Golf Association)

Tom Weiskopf, the enormously talented tall man, his greatness re-
strained only by a temperament that defied control.

Johnny Miller, the golden gun of the West, who could shoot lights
out anywhere. Like, for instance, a final-round 63 in the 1973 Open
at rugged Oakmont.

Raymond Floyd, a reformed playboy who set many a social endurance record and had also tied Nicklaus for the Masters scoring record earlier in the year.

And Hubert Green, at the time the tour's leading money winner. He had put together a rare sweep of three consecutive titles earlier in the season.

John Mahaffey, who almost won in 1975, was in the field, as was Lou Graham, who did win, and British Open champion Tom Watson.

So, too, were some of the fuzzy-cheeked ones such as Tom Kite, Ben Crenshaw, and, yes, Jerome Kendrick Pate.

However, Nicklaus was getting most of the attention.

"He's the greatest player of all time, doubt it not," said Weiskopf, an Ohio State Buckeye like Jack, but who always played in his shadow. "He is the favorite. He's the favorite every time he tees it up. When you get to the major championships, he's even more of a favorite. He's the man you have to beat."

So Nicklaus went out and opened with a four-over-par 74.

Meanwhile, quiet, short-hitting Mike Reid, a twenty-one-year-old senior at Brigham Young University, slipped in with 67, the only player under par.

Pate actually had the lead at one point on opening day, playing to two under through eight holes, but he took bogeys on Nos. 9 and 10 late in the day.

"I just got tired, emotionally drained after the first nine holes," he said later. "I didn't tee off until 2:32. It was after 5:00 when we made the turn."

Pate wound up the first day with a credible 71. Green, a Birmingham native, had 72.

Pate's one-over score came with an unusual circumstance that caused a bogey on No. 18. It's a hole he'll never forget, but not for that first-round reason. His story would be complete three days hence.

He had just cleared the pond when a disturbed bullfrog mashed his ball down in the grass. Pate could barely dislodge it, but he managed to get up and down in two more strokes for bogey.

"The USGA official said he didn't have enough evidence to give me a free drop," said Pate, "but people in the stands said they saw it."

Mahaffey, the victim to Lou Graham in the previous Open at Medinah in Chicago, was always labeled one of the finest ball strikers on tour, and he showed it with a fine second-round 68 to take the lead at 138. Al Geiberger came in at 70-69—139.

Pate could have shared the lead but bogeyed Nos. 17 and 18, both caused by three-putts.

"I sorta fell asleep on those two," he confessed. "But I've always played the tough courses well. And, believe me, this one is tough."

Green hung in with 70 for 142.

Then came Saturday . . . and the thunder and rain. The third round was delayed two hours because of the storm, and USGA officials were very near considering going to a thirty-six-hole windup for Sunday.

The grim Mahaffey, who had vowed to make up for the previous year's disappointment, had to wait until 4:29 (EST) to tee off in his quest. He finished in the gloaming at 8:35 P.M., but he played in with 69 for a two-stroke lead over Pate. The two would be in the final pairing on Sunday. Headline stuff.

Pate also shot 69, but he did it the hard way.

He was four over par through only four holes and seemingly severely leaking oil. But he came back. How he came back!

Hitching up his belt, he birdied three of the next four holes to erase much of the deficit, then scored an impressive eagle three on No. 12.

Speaking of his disastrous Saturday start, Pate said he wasn't overly tight or tense, "I just didn't have good feel."

He felt good Saturday evening.

"I think there's less pressure in being two back than two ahead," he said.

Well grilled by the press, Mahaffey, a protégé of Ben Hogan in his native Texas, had won just once on tour.

"Am I mentally tough enough now to win this thing?" he asked himself. "We'll find out."

So, on Open Sunday, off they went, Mahaffey and Pate, and the Texan held his own through most of the day, but it wasn't all day.

The five-iron shot, *that* five iron, would be the most memorable of the tournament, but Pate later felt like he won his spurs on the rugged, 215-yard par-three fifteenth. There he laced in a one iron and the ball spun off the slope to within six feet. He holed for a birdie two.

He was within one.

Then Mahaffey bogeyed the sixteenth. Tie game. He then three-putted from across the green, and for the first time in the tournament Pate had the lead.

Normally played as a par five, the eighteenth was set up for a killer par four for the Open. Pate drove into the right rough, Mahaffey across the fairway in the high grass to the left. Wee John had to try for it with a wood from the rough. He had to go for it. Water! But it was his only choice.

Pate had a more than decent lie and was 190 yards away. Adrenaline overflowing, he pulled a five iron from the bag and looked at a pin placed precariously near the water on the left. The next step was one of the most spectacular shots in U.S. Open history. It landed three feet from the hole, to the left.

The ever-calm Pate called over USGA president Harry Easterly and P. J. Boatwright, the tournament director, to make certain he had that one-shot lead. They confirmed it. All he had to do was two-putt from three feet to win.

"I hadn't been nervous all day until then," remembers Pate. "Then I didn't know if I was burning up or freezing to death. At least I didn't drop the putter. I don't know if I could have picked it up." But he firmed it right in there.

As far as could be confirmed, it was the first time a player had birdied the seventy-second hole to win the Open.

"This is the greatest moment of my life," said the champion, the sweat fighting through his Alabama-red golf shirt. "I'm twenty-two and I've won the Open. I can't believe it."

Vinny Giles, the former amateur champion turned sports agent,

Pate embracing golf official and good friend Elbert
Jemison Jr. after winning the U.S. Open (Courtesy U.S.
Golf Association)

was off to the side observing. "He's going to be one of the all-time
great players," he said.

Later that year Pate closed the Canadian Open with a resounding
63 and beat Jack Nicklaus to win there. He would win the Players
Championship and cause more than a ripple when he pushed commissioner Deane Beman and architect Pete Dye into the water at the
TPC course at Sawgrass and then dived in himself.

But a shoulder injury began dragging down his playing career, and with a forced limited schedule he became less of a factor.

That five iron, not the swan dive, made him famous. He has been kidded that one day, on his deathbed, he would finally admit he pulled that five iron. After all, he had a mile of freedom to the safer right side.

"I had the perfect angle coming from that right rough to have a straight shot at the flag. It was a perfect setup."

Anyway, the ambitious Pate plunged into the business world of golf. He'd always had a penchant for construction work and course design, closely observing the building of Jack Nicklaus–designed Shoal Creek in Birmingham.

He did some consulting work with Tom Fazio at Bluewater Bay in Niceville, Florida, and that was to be the first of several projects he would complete with the renowned architect.

Pate was now on his own, and he could well stand on his own. He was involved with more than twenty courses, including much-applauded ones such as Dancing Rabbit in Mississippi, Kiva Dunes on the Gulf Coast, and Limestone Springs near Birmingham.

Jerry Pate Turf and Irrigation distributes Toro equipment in the Southeast, and in the year 2001 he got back to some fairly serious golf playing.

He returned to Atlanta to play on exemption in the 2001 PGA, twenty-five years after he won the Open. Pate caught everyone's attention in the second round. He was five under through fourteen holes, but a couple of bad breaks and misdeeds on the seventeenth and eighteenth cost him. He double-bogeyed both, shot 70, and missed the cut by one.

Later in the year, playing in a charity event at Old Overton in Birmingham, a course he designed with Fazio, he went around in a flawless 62 with nine birdies and nine pars. He looked as smooth as a young Jerry Pate.

At age forty-eight he looked at another chapter. He will definitely play the senior tour. Business is good, the kids are gone, the shoulder's fine, so it's time to play some golf again.

There was one other principal highlight in 2001. Asked at that year's Open if he was a graduate of the University of Alabama, he replied, "No, pro golf was too tempting, but someday I'm gonna get that degree."

In 2001 he put on that cap and gown along with another member of his family, his daughter Jennifer.

19

The Night Hank Aaron Outhomered Babe Ruth

WAYNE MARTIN

APRIL IN ATLANTA CAN BE as gentle as a caress, as soothing and light as a baby's breath against your neck.

But April in Atlanta also can have a bite. Frosty mornings can burn the azaleas. And the smell as you head south toward Macon can be the eye-stinging smoke from smudgepots used as weapons against killing frostbite on delicate peach blossoms.

It was the chilly, damp bite of Atlanta that greeted Hank Aaron and the Atlanta Braves on April 8, 1974. After opening the season with three games in Cincinnati, the Braves were at Atlanta–Fulton County Stadium for their Monday home opener. It had rained that day and a

Much of this account was reconstructed from the late Alf Van Hoose's memorable on-the-scene report for the *Birmingham News*. Had Hank Aaron's record-breaking home run come a day later, Alf would have been in Augusta covering the Masters and Wayne Martin would have been in the Atlanta press box that night for the *News*.

cold wind cut through the jacketed sportswriters, many of whom were stopping off in Atlanta before going on to the Masters golf tournament in Augusta.

The cold, damp night usually meant more empty seats than full ones in Atlanta. But on this occasion people packed every seat and others stood along the concourse openings hoping for a glimpse at baseball history.

Braves outfielder Hank Aaron had hit career home run No. 714 four nights earlier in Cincinnati. It came after an edict from Commissioner Bowie Kuhn that Aaron would play, and it had tied Aaron with Babe Ruth for most career home runs, a record many had felt would never be broken.

Braves owner Bill Bartholemay had said Aaron would not play in Cincinnati, hoping thus to save Aaron's final assault on Ruth's record for Atlanta fans. But Kuhn's decree to field manager Eddie Mathews overruled the Braves boss. Aaron's first swing of the season, at Riverfront Stadium, had pulled him even with the Babe.

Hank sat out the next game, but after another Kuhn order he was back in the lineup for the series finale on Sunday. Aaron failed to produce the go-ahead homer in Cincinnati. Twice he was called out on strikes in an 0-for-3 evening. Then back in Atlanta he strongly defended himself against critics who hinted that he had given less than his best against Cincinnati pitching on Sunday. Aaron said that wasn't the way he played, not since his sandlot days in Mobile, Alabama. He gave it his best, he insisted.

The first sandlots for the boy who would become the greatest home-run hitter of them all were more swamp than sand in a section near Mobile called Down the Bay. Today, it would be a ghetto. Then it was a neighborhood where blacks raised their families after many had left Alabama's Black Belt farms for the lure of jobs in Mobile shipyards.

With defense-related companies hiring, Herbert and Estelle Aaron moved their growing family from rural Camden in Wilcox

County to Mobile. Herbert worked in the shipyards, and the family grew. First came Sarah, then Herbert Jr., Henry, Gloria, Tommie, Alfred, and Alfreda.

Henry was born on February 5, 1934. When he was nine years old, his father took advantage of good pay in the middle of World War II to move his family to the Toulminville section of Mobile. Henry once said that his father used discarded lumber to build their house in a section of unpaved streets and open space in which children could play.

A part of that open space became Carver Park, across the street from the Aaron house. Henry once said that access to the park helped him sharpen the skills he would use to chase, catch, and pass Babe Ruth.

Perhaps Aaron gave more credit to the park than was due. It was more of a playground than a real baseball park; the only organized activity offered was softball. Aaron played some football in high school, but baseball wasn't an option—except in his dreams.

Although Mobile lacked youth organizations for black children, baseball facilities, or formal coaching, the city and surrounding areas were a gold mine of baseball talent. Billy Williams, Aaron, and Willie McCovey made it to Cooperstown. Add to that trio Hank's brother Tommie (who played with him at Milwaukee and Atlanta), Tommie Agee, Cleon Jones, and Amos Otis, and Mobile's credentials as an incubator of baseball greats are solid.

Along with the black players, the Mobile area can boast of Milt and Frank Bolling and, in later years, Dave Stapleton.

It was from this environment that Hank Aaron exploded, first as a sixteen-year-old with the Mobile Black Bears. At first, Hank's mother forbade baseball for her son. Baseball was played on Sunday and Henry would not play on Sunday, she said. But with persistence, Henry helped wear down her objection with the promise that he would earn two dollars a game. The possibility of his eventually earning a real living playing baseball convinced his mother that perhaps Hank might be permitted to go away to play with the Indianapolis Clowns of the Negro National League. Thus he left Mobile before graduating from high school, promising his mother that that would come later.

Once he was on the road, there was no stopping the kid from Mobile. His talent couldn't be concealed; soon Aaron was sold to the Milwaukee Braves, and his climb up the baseball ladder had begun.

First, Aaron broke the color line in Eau Claire, Wisconsin. He did it again the next year in Jacksonville, Florida, and then he joined Milwaukee in 1954. Ultimately he went to the batter's box at Atlanta–Fulton County Stadium on a chilly April night twenty years and 714 homers after joining the Braves.

Hank Aaron awoke on that Monday in Atlanta to gray skies. Rain fell early in the day, then the sun came out. But cold weather was due in early evening, and with it the possibility of more rain.

That night a damp, chilly wind invaded the stadium. In the third inning rain fell and sleet threatened, reported *Birmingham News* sports editor Alf Van Hoose. But it seemed, he wrote, that the calm, determined Aaron, who had suffered an entire winter waiting after hitting homer No. 713 late in 1973, almost willed the weather to hold off. "I'd have gone out and put that tarp down myself after the fourth (inning)," Aaron would say later.

Stadium gates had opened early for the record 53,775 who came hoping to witness history. Pearl Bailey sang the National Anthem, and Sammy Davis Jr. offered $25,000 for the home-run ball if Aaron connected.

The Los Angeles Dodgers batted first, against Ron Reed, and the crowd appeared uninterested.

When Hank Aaron walked toward the plate in the second inning, a buzz began in the crowd, grew, and then quieted.

Aaron's gait as he moved out to take his bat was not a swagger; it showed no determination, no authority. It was more of a stroll, the deliberate pace that earlier in his career had earned him the nickname "Snowshoe."

He had pursued Babe Ruth's record in much the same way he now sauntered to the plate: low-key and seemingly in the shadow of more flashy players. Others seemed to play baseball like the brass section of an orchestra, bringing crowds to their feet in a frenzy of excitement and emotion. Aaron played the game like a soft background melody, seemingly unnoticed but always there playing his part.

Other players reaped big money from endorsements and negotiating huge salaries at contract renewal time. Aaron labored quietly. His salary rose, of course, but comparatively few endorsements had fallen into the lap of the quiet man from Mobile.

Now, with helmet in one hand and two bats held firmly in the other, he appeared relaxed as he made his way to the plate. His routine was the same as always: he stopped just outside the batter's box, discarded one bat, and leaned the other against a leg while he wiggled his batting helmet firmly onto his head.

Only then did he step into the batter's box, still in a relaxed, almost disinterested manner, almost as though his mind were far away.

But Aaron's mind was where the battle for homer No. 715 had begun the night before, on the flight from Cincinnati. He would say later, "I started thinking of (pitcher) Al Downing . . . on the way home from Cincinnati. Basically, I knew what he would like me to hit—his fastball, which tails away and, if he's right, is his best pitch."

Aaron was a student of pitchers. Sometimes he would sit in the dugout, holding his cap in front of his face, and focus on the pitcher through the small vent hole in the cap, shutting out the crowd and the other players and making that pitcher the center of his consciousness.

He would study the pitcher's moves, refreshing his memory of past meetings. "A good pitcher usually has three pitches," Aaron once said. "I decide which one I know he will throw, and then I wait for that pitch."

So, the mind is one weapon against the enemy on the mound. It's a companion to the weapon of patience. And patience was a way of life for Hank Aaron.

Aaron's passion had been to play with the best, but to do that would take patience. Black players, no matter how good, couldn't play in the major leagues, some people still thought back then. Ask Josh Gibson, or Cool Papa Bell, or Birmingham's Piper Davis, who most people thought would have been a great one—if only he had been born a little later.

For those blacks, patience meant waiting for a chance to play with the Indianapolis Clowns or the Birmingham Black Barons or the Mobile Black Bears. But because of one man, Jackie Robinson, Hank Aaron's patience meant a change in the major leagues.

Robinson had opened the door and made it possible for the dream of little Henry Aaron to come true. It took men with special talents and special patience to step through the door Robinson had opened when he signed with the Brooklyn Dodgers and became the first African American in the Major Leagues.

Aaron's first tentative steps through the door had come with a train ride to join the Indianapolis Clowns. He recalled that he had two dollars, a little food his mother had packed, and a cardboard suitcase.

He had made the trip as he would make trips to the batter's box: calmly and without fanfare. Patience was paying off, but was there enough talent, enough strength?

Aaron had been sold to the Milwaukee Braves, and he reported to Eau Claire, Wisconsin, as an infielder. His second year he broke the color line in Jacksonville, Florida, in the South Atlantic League. There is the story—fact or myth—that when he left Mobile he was batting crosshanded and didn't change until he received professional coaching.

But there was no doubting the talent. Others could play shortstop and second base better, but the way Aaron handled the bat meant that a place had to be made for him. He became an outfielder. He worked hard to learn playing the outfield, and when he played in the majors he became a Golden Glove outfielder.

So, he had the patience and talent, but what about strength?

Before the days of steroids and weight training, few baseball players had massive physiques. Weight training was discouraged because it was felt that excess muscles hampered swings.

Aaron's physical appearance turned few heads. But he did turn heads when he swung a bat.

Don Drysdale, the Los Angeles Dodger pitcher who gave up more Aaron home runs (seventeen) than any other pitcher, remembered a homer Aaron hit in the LA Coliseum. "It's bad enough," Drysdale said, "to have him hit any home run off you and wonder: How far is that one going? But with that Aaron homer in the Coliseum, I ended up with not only mental anguish, but literally physical pain." Drysdale said Aaron hit the ball so hard and he turned his head so fast to watch its flight that he actually jerked a crick in his neck.

So, Aaron had patience and strength. Now what he needed was opportunity.

Al Downing was the man fate chose to provide that opportunity. (Perhaps Downing saw it simply as the luck of the draw—his turn to pitch that night in Atlanta.)

"He knows what I can throw," Downing had said in sizing up the situation. "I'm not going to change my pattern for him. I mustn't go against what I've been successful with. If I throw 715, I'm not going to run and hide. On the other hand, I'm not going to run to the plate to congratulate him."

The pressure of the moment was almost a physical thing that could be touched and felt.

On Aaron's first trip to the plate that night he had had no opportunity for homer 715. Downing had walked him on four pitches, and the fans sat back, burrowing a little deeper into their jackets and blankets. They would just have to wait on Aaron's next at-bat or perhaps the one after that.

When Aaron returned to the plate in the fourth inning, two men were out and Darrell Evans was on first base. Again, Downing's first pitch was a ball, this one in the dirt. That made five straight balls to Aaron, and the crowd was heard grumbling between pitches.

The first-base umpire had a supply of specially marked balls to ensure that, in the event Aaron homered, the ball he hit could be readily identified. The ump tossed a new ball to Downing and the fans went silent, moving to the edges of their seats as the pitcher went into his windup.

Downing's sixth delivery would have been another ball had Aaron not swung. That swing produced what the crowd had waited for and what forty-year-old Hank Aaron had been waiting almost twenty years to make.

The ball rose and sailed toward left field. More than one of the golf-oriented sportswriters (very soon to cover the Masters) would, in their next morning's editions, describe Aaron's swing as similar to a perfect four-iron shot.

Every eye in the stadium watched, and one pair of hands waited just over the fence in left center. Bullpen pitchers had been stationed at intervals between the fence and the stands in case the ball didn't make it out of the park. This one made it just far enough and into the glove of pitcher Tom House. He soon delivered the ball into Aaron's hands at home plate. And baseball had a new career home-run king.

Escorted by two fans who had run onto the field, Aaron crossed the plate and into the waiting celebration—first with his family, then his teammates, then President Nixon (by phone), then the nation.

What was the Downing pitch that Aaron had hit? On that chilly April night in Atlanta, Hank said it was a fastball that drifted into the strike zone—just what he'd been looking for. Downing said it was a fastball, but not a good one. He said he'd never felt in rhythm that night.

Aaron hammers his 714th homer in Cincinnati, tying Babe Ruth.
(Courtesy Atlanta Baseball Club)

(In an anniversary interview twenty-five years later, Aaron would say the pitch was a high slider out over the plate.)

Both Aaron and Downing said the pitch location was not what the pitcher wanted, another case of a batter taking advantage of a pitcher's mistake, as happens with most home runs. Both hitters and pitchers usually attribute a home run to the hitter's jumping on a mistake. But there are mistakes that pitchers get away with, and probably some perfect pitches that end up as home runs.

Surely some of Aaron's 755 home runs came off good pitches. Sometimes the hitter takes on a good pitch and wins the battle.

Thus, whether on this night it was a mistake or a perfect pitch, it became Aaron home run No. 715. Some who knew Aaron best said they saw something that night they seldom had seen: a grin on the face of the man who always played the game dead seriously.

When the game was over (Atlanta won 7–4), the stadium emptied. Aaron, recounting the record homer, said he enjoyed hitting No. 715 more than 714 because 714 had come in a loss, whereas this one helped the Braves win. But, chances are, most of the people watching had little concern about winning or losing because probably few of the seats were held by faithful fans. Most seats belonged to people who came to witness history.

Aaron went on to finish his career with the Milwaukee Brewers, hitting forty more home runs before hanging it up. He stayed in baseball as an executive with the Braves in Atlanta.

The home-run king looked back on the events of 1973 and 1974 with mixed feelings. He remembered the relief of getting the burden of chasing history off his back—and he remembered the feeling of accomplishment.

He also remembered the hate letters he had received and the threats to his family. He recalled the bodyguards who were assigned to him, protectors he thinks wouldn't have been necessary had the player chasing Babe Ruth's record been white.

But he also looked back with a feeling of pride and accomplishment because the door that Jackie Robinson had unlocked, Hank Aaron had thrown wide open.

20

Golf's Toughest Day . . . and Under a Gun!

JIM MARTIN

THE GRITTY, HIGH-STRUNG HUBERT GREEN likes to eat pressure for breakfast. Back in his halcyon days, the mid-1970s, he would order it on a regular basis.

Many who had studied Green agreed that he always put too much pressure on himself.

One person who commented was Arnold Palmer. "I always thought Hubert was a very good player," said Palmer, "but I always thought he was hurting himself by talking like that."

A routine that Green used over and over was this: "When it came time to stand up in the majors, I've always sat down."

Coming into the 1977 U.S. Open at Southern Hills in Tulsa, Green's best finish in a major was a tie for third in the 1974 PGA at Tanglewood in North Carolina.

But this was a week in a June cauldron when he stood up and reached his full height. It would go down as one of the most historic U.S. Open championships. For a lot of reasons.

The thirty-one-year-old Green was at his peak. He had led the money list for a good portion of 1976 and had, in fact, won three consecutive tournaments in the spring: Doral, Jacksonville, and the Heritage Classic at Hilton Head.

Never at a loss for words, Green continued to talk about his reasoning. "I do put more pressure on myself than anyone else," he said. "Frankly, it makes me play better. I do it on purpose, more than normal. I talk about choking."

The Southern Hills course was truly a magnificent test for the 1977 Open, annually ranked by *Golf Digest* as one of the nation's top ten courses. The course was designed during the Depression by Perry Maxwell, who also laid out the famed Colonial in Fort Worth. The No. 1 and No. 10 holes flow from one of the highest points in Tulsa—you can easily see the city's skyline ten miles away through gently rolling valleys.

It is a driver's course, comfortable for the precise Green.

Not so for an erratic tee-shot man like Ben Crenshaw.

One morning, holding court, the likable Texan said he was going to have surgery on his nose to give his allergies some relief. Someone asked him what type of allergies were bothering him.

"Moss, trees, moguls, grass . . . especially deep rough."

The defending champion was Jerry Pate of Alabama connections, who had won the Open in 1976 at Atlanta Athletic Club.

Since 1920 only Bobby Jones (1929–30), Ralph Guldahl (1937–38), and Ben Hogan (1950–51) had repeated in the Open, but that didn't faze the brash young Pate.

"I don't think there's a jinx or anything," he said. "Somebody twenty or under wasn't supposed to win the U.S. Amateur, but I did. Somebody twenty-two wasn't supposed to win the U.S. Open, but I did. There's no reason I can't do it again."

But Pate wouldn't defend; he wouldn't even make the cut. He'd been fighting a shoulder inflammation all year and would shoot 72-76—148 and bow out.

But that Open trophy would have room for some additional Alabama fingerprints.

Green could correctly call himself the first-round leader, with a one-under-par 69, but so could six others in the heavy traffic. They were Rod Funseth, Terry Diehl, Larry Nelson, Grier Jones, Tom Purtzer, and your token one-round Open flash, Florentino Molina.

That almost went unnoticed because of a guy named Palmer. On the 614-yard fifth, Arnie was about to hurt himself. His three-wood third shot (that's right, third) was thirty yards short of the green. He then holed his pitch for birdie, and you could have heard the roar all the way to Texas. Palmer had a 70 and said ruefully afterward, "This is the kind of score I used to shoot in the Open."

The first-round 71 by Terrible Tom Weiskopf was most interesting. He started with a double bogey ("I was hot"), parred the second, and then made triple bogey on No. 3 ("You should have seen me then"), but he brought it back with four birdies, all tough ones.

"Is that the best comeback you've ever made?" someone asked him.

"It probably is," he grinned. "All the other times I've done that before I've walked in off the course."

"Well, I qualified," said Green of his opening 69.

Friday was even better. It was so hot, statues were sweating. Palmer and Jack Nicklaus wore white floppy hats.

"It didn't bother me," Green told the nation's press. "I'm from Birmingham. We have a little of this down there, too."

Friday was a day to enjoy for Hubert as he brought in a 67 for 136 and a one-stroke lead.

Although his score was lower than on opening day, it wasn't nearly as solid a round. He saved himself with that old green-gripped putter that had nearly gained folklore status.

"It was made by the Great Lakes Golf Company in December of 1930," he quipped. "They went out of business in January of 1931."

He used only twelve putts on Friday's front nine for a 32, but he had scattered drives all over the lot.

"I'm enjoying all of this," he said. "Everyone is going to ask me if I'm going to take the gas. I've led before in major championships and I haven't won. I won Philadelphia in '74 and Palm Springs, but who remembers? They remember a major winner.

"I don't want to relax and I don't intend to. I want to improve my position. I want two sub-par rounds. If I get that someone may still beat me. If they do, I'll be back next year."

What else did he enjoy in addition to the one-stroke lead over Diehl (69-68—137)? "Well," said Hubert, "the butterflies, my stomach sinking, the aggravation of autograph signing, the questions of the press, and the thrill of the hunt."

After two rounds it was still very much crowded. Unlikelies Purtzer (138), lefty Sam Adams, and Rod Funseth were joined by Gary Player at 139. Player had a part in the highlight film on No. 9. En route to a 67, his second shot hit the cart path and bounded into the high rough on the hill side of the No. 1 tee fifty yards away. Incredibly, he holed the pitch for a birdie three.

Green went over par for the first time in the tournament with a two-over-par 72, but he still managed to hold a one-stroke lead. He had been at the top all the way. A long, long, pressurized week.

He started with bogeys on two of the first three holes but hung in, determined to reach a "personal, private goal."

"Momentum, I don't believe in that," he said. "I know I've got to play good golf Sunday. If I shoot 75, I'm not going to win. But if I shoot 68, somebody's going to have to shoot an awfully good score.

"I am concerned about Hubert Green. No one else.

"I try to stay on the same even keel. You have to in an Open championship. If you let a bogey upset you, or a birdie put you too high, then you're going to have problems. You just have to wait. You have to be patient. Particularly on this golf course. I don't feel bad about 72. This is the Open. You don't burn up this golf course every day."

Green stood at 208 after three rounds. Andy Bean came with a 68, lowering his scores every day, and was in at 209. Purtzer, Player,

Weiskopf, and unknowns Gary Jacobson and Don Padgett, son of the then-PGA president, were all at 210.

Then came Open Sunday, the most draining day in all of golf, at least for those who had a chance. There didn't even used to be an Open Sunday. The USGA would close with thirty-six holes on Saturday, but Ken Venturi's near–heat collapse at Congressional in Washington in 1964 changed all that. He white-eyed his way somehow to the championship, and the board soon voted to eliminate that type of finish. From now on it would be eighteen on Sunday.

It would provide the ultimate in high theater for the U.S. Open. In 1973 Johnny Miller came roaring down the way with a last-round 63 to win at Oakmont. Pate would, of course, strike that famous five iron at the final hole to win the 1976 Open at Atlanta.

But this 1977 deal at Tulsa would not be forgotten.

Green teed off in the company of Bean, Florida State versus Florida, Bean being the Gator, but this was far from a college match. Hubert got an early edge when Bean three-putted No. 1. Green made an unbelievable save for par at the second, then holed birdie putts on Nos. 3 and 4, both of them uphill, which is the only way to putt on the slick surfaces at Southern Hills.

Then Green bogeyed the ninth and tenth holes about the time the normally quiet Lou Graham, the 1975 Open champion, began making noises. Graham had birdies on Nos. 12, 14, 15, and 16, and a miraculous recovery from the woods gave him a five-foot birdie attempt for a fourth straight at the seventeenth.

But Green was about to encounter far more serious troubles of his own on the fifteenth.

He had received a death threat: technically, the USGA had.

The rest of this piece will be basically told by Frank D. "Sandy" Tatum, the eloquent San Francisco attorney who was then president of the USGA, and by Green himself.

"Word came from security when Hubert was on the tenth hole," explained Tatum, "that there was a death threat involving Hubert Green.

A woman said she had three friends who had been in trouble and had every intent to get in more trouble and she wanted to save them.

"We checked security and we decided that it was not only more than adequate, but impressive. But we had to make a decision. Should we say anything to Hubert? It was a most difficult choice. The odds were overwhelming that nothing would happen, but we felt that it was not our decision when a man's personal safety might be involved.

"We could have chosen to suspend play, we had other alternatives," he continued. "Finally, as Hubert finished play on the fourteenth green, we decided to tell him. In light of Lou Graham's charge and the pressure of the entire situation, a lesser man might not have been able to respond.

"I cannot tell you, in light of what happened today, what I think of Hubert Green. I have never dealt with a man like that.

"Courage was once described as grace under pressure. If indeed that is the proper description, I think it is never more applicable than today in the case of Hubert."

Once informed, Green said "Let's go," then hit an uncharacteristic hook off that very tee. He told his caddy, Shane Grier, "Don't walk too close to me." He then dug an eight iron out of the rough and two-putted downhill from forty feet for his par. He followed with a birdie on the par-five sixteenth, sliding a wedge within two feet of the cup.

"I know this is news," said Green, "but let's don't blow it out of proportion. I'd rather you write about me winning the Open. I had enough problems on the fifteenth hole just trying to make par."

After Graham missed his birdie at the seventeenth, Green got his par. He had a two-shot margin going to the uphill eighteenth. He drove perfectly, just where he wanted, and put his second into the front left bunker, just where he didn't want to be.

"I didn't want to put it there, but that's exactly what I did. Any place but there. I had been practicing long bunker shots all week and I said, 'Don't leave it short,' but I did. Then I said, 'Don't leave the putt short,' but I did.

Birmingham's Hubert Green swings confidently, especially under pressure. (Courtesy U.S. Golf Association)

"But I survived. And I guess that's what you do when you win the Open. You survive."

Green had rounds of 69-67-72-70 for 278. Graham closed with a pair of 68s for 279, and Weiskopf finished third at 281.

Engulfed by applause at the eighteenth hole and surrounded by heavy security, Green clutched the Open trophy and said, "I just looked down at the names on this trophy and saw Walter Hagen's name on it. That's the first one I saw. I can't tell you how proud I am that my name will be added to this. I hope I'm honorable enough to be a worthy champion."

Hubert wrote one of the most memorable stories of all those Opens, but he was far from finished. He would say a year or so later, "If my goal was to win just one major, I wouldn't have anything left to attain. You need something to duplicate the one before it.

"It's just like popcorn. You can't eat just one handful."

He would get him some more popcorn.

In 1978 he went to Cherry Hills in Denver to defend his Open championship. He didn't make the cut, but he was there in 1985 for the PGA Championship and whipped playing partner Lee Trevino to win in a classic face-to-face showdown. He would later say that that major meant even more, for it proved he could do it again.

Recently, Jerry Pate said of his friend Hubert, "He has the best golf mind of anyone I've ever been around, including Jack Nicklaus. When he saw that I had won the Open, he damn sure knew he could do it."

21

Heisman Double for Auburn

PHILLIP MARSHALL

IT STARTED AS ROUTINE APPLAUSE. As Bo Jackson stepped back from the podium at New York's hallowed Downtown Athletic Club, the applause grew louder. Finally, audience members were standing, applauding, and cheering.

The day was December 13, 1985. The poor kid from Bessemer who once had seemed almost certainly headed for reform school was now standing at the top of the college football world, proclaimed the best player in the land.

Bo was the eighth of Florence Bond's ten children. He grew up in a little house in Bessemer. Now, here he was decked out in a tuxedo and accepting the most coveted award in college sports.

"My mom raised us in a three-room house," Jackson told those gathered to honor him. "The house consisted of a kitchen, where my mom had her bedroom; a living room, which had a gas heater; and a bedroom that had a potbellied stove and twin beds.

"As children, we slept wherever we could find a vacant place in the house. And the majority of the time I would get down right in front of the little gas heater in the living room. Some nights I didn't have a cover to put over me, but I knew my mom would take care of me."

Nothing in football, Jackson said, could compare with the warmth he felt when his mother came in the night and covered him with a blanket.

"I don't care about all the criticism people throw at me because I know I've had harder times," Jackson said. "Nothing can make me feel better than what I've experienced growing up."

Fourteen years earlier on that same stage, another Auburn hero had stepped forward. Quarterback Pat Sullivan graciously became Auburn's first Heisman Trophy winner.

They were very different people in very different times, but Sullivan and Jackson each had lifted Auburn football in his own way.

Jackson was the catalyst who helped Auburn coach Pat Dye embark on the greatest decade in Auburn football history. Sullivan and red-haired wide receiver Terry Beasley led a transformation into the modern ways of offensive football.

Sullivan and later Jackson were at their best in what might have seemed the bleakest of times.

Auburn athletics director David Housel recalled, "Coach Dye said of Bo Jackson that he gave Auburn people the greatest thing in the world. He gave them hope—hope of beating Alabama, hope of building a championship football program.

"I think the same could be said of Pat Sullivan. And in Auburn history, it is impossible to talk of Pat Sullivan without talking about receiver Terry Beasley. Together they gave Auburn hope that Auburn never had had at that time in our history."

Jackson, 222 powerful pounds with the speed of a world-class sprinter, won the Heisman Trophy by rushing for 1,786 yards as a senior in 1985. He went on to be a star in baseball for the Kansas City Royals and Chicago White Sox and in football for the Oakland Raiders. Before a hip injury cut his career short, he was a Nike marketing icon.

At McAdory High School near Bessemer, Bo was Mr. Everything

in sports, once scoring twenty-nine points in a football game and batting just under .500 in baseball. Ronald Weathers, veteran of the high school sports beat, recalled that in a state meet Jackson had the decathlon won after nine of the nine events, so he bypassed the mile run, the scheduled tenth.

In 1982, as a shy freshman, Jackson electrified the Auburn football program when he turned down a $250,000 bonus offer to play baseball for the New York Yankees, choosing instead to play football for Auburn.

Bobby Wallace, the assistant Auburn coach who recruited Bo, knew of Bo's potential even before Jackson arrived on campus. So did Coach Dye. But after the first preseason scrimmage it seemed that everyone at Auburn knew.

"I'll never forget that scrimmage in the stadium where Bo ran wild," Wallace said. "There was electricity in the air. The coaches could feel it, and you could see it in the players' eyes. Everybody knew this guy was something different, the real thing."

For Jackson, the burden was heavy. As he neared the end of his freshman year, he decided he had "had enough"—enough of the expectations, enough of school, enough of everything. Between Auburn's games against Georgia and Alabama, Bo went to the bus station in Opelika. He wanted to go home.

One bus left, then another and another. But Bo never got on one. Finally, at 1:30 in the morning, he phoned Wallace.

"I was sound asleep, but I woke up quick," Wallace later recounted. "I just told Bo to go on back to the dorm and go to sleep, that I would take care of things. We worked it out the next day. Bo got his punishment like any of the other players would have, and there was never any problem after that."

Jackson's punishment was one hundred "stadiums"—climbing to the top of Jordan-Hare Stadium and back one hundred times. A few days later he rushed for 114 yards and went over the top for the winning touchdown as Auburn ended ten years of frustration with a 23–22 victory over Alabama.

Even as Jackson became a nationally acclaimed football player, pil-

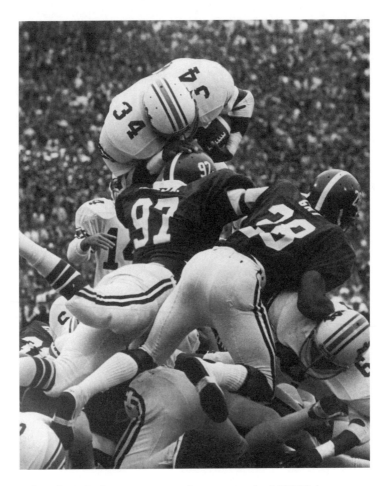

Auburn's Bo Jackson goes over the top—to the 1985 Heisman
Trophy. (Courtesy Auburn University)

ing up yards and touchdowns and leading Auburn to the 1983 Southeastern Conference championship, his road was bumpy. Slowed by a
bad ankle, in the second game of the season he suffered a separated
shoulder against Texas and missed six games. Against Alabama, with
the game on the line, he was supposed to block for Brent Fullwood
out of the wishbone with victory only feet away. But Bo went the
wrong way, Fullwood was stopped, and Auburn lost.

In his Heisman year Bo endured stinging criticism after removing himself from games against Tennessee and Florida because of injuries; Auburn lost to both.

But Coach Dye staunchly defended him. "Bo has always been a man who never looked back," he said. "He hasn't ever had to make any apologies either. That includes when he went the wrong way on the goal line and we lost to Alabama, and when he came out of a couple of games because he got hurt. He caught some flak from a lot of people who didn't know what the hell they were talking about."

Jackson had gone into his senior year as the clear Heisman favorite, but criticism took its toll, and Iowa quarterback Chuck Long was closing in fast. Playing on a bum ankle, Jackson rushed for 121 yards and made the game-turning touchdown on a sixty-seven-yard spectacular run against Georgia. He caught two passes for forty-eight yards and a touchdown that was just enough.

The Tampa Bay Bucs made Jackson the first player chosen in the NFL draft, but he shocked the sports world by opting to play baseball with the Kansas City Royals. He became a major league star, hitting gargantuan home runs, including one in the Major League All-Star Game. Then he went back to football and ran for the Raiders as he had run for Auburn.

Jackson had a penchant for the spectacular, whether in football, baseball, or track. Auburn track coach Mel Rosen said that if Bo had focused on track he would have been an Olympic gold medal contender. After his injury, Jackson had hip replacement surgery and became the first professional athlete ever to return to play after such an injury. After his return, he hit a home run in his first at-bat.

But Jackson never liked fame. When he retired in 1994, he left happily. He chose to live in suburban Chicago with his wife and three children. He is president of the Sports Medicine Council of Health-South.

"People ask me all the time if I remember this game or that game. Of if I remember when I did a particular thing," Jackson said. "But all those things are in the past. My career wasn't cut short by injury.

My career was cut short because I *wanted* it to end. I don't miss it at all."

Bo's exploits are still the stuff of legend at Auburn. In the school's football complex, a picture of Jackson going over the top against Alabama in 1982 occupies a place of honor. His and Sullivan's Heisman Trophies are on display for all to see.

By twenty-first-century standards, Pat Sullivan's statistics aren't overly impressive, but they were plenty impressive when he finished his career in 1971. He tied an NCAA record with a touchdown responsibility of seventy-one. His fifty-three career touchdown passes were third best in NCAA history. His total offense of 228.1 yards per game set an NCAA record.

More than numbers on paper, though, Sullivan left a legacy of leadership. He welcomed the burden carried by those called on to show the way.

"I've never seen Pat worried, not even when we're behind," fullback Wallace Clark said as Sullivan headed into his senior season. "Concerned? Yes. Worried? No. He knows how to win, how to come back when he gets behind. And he always keeps the pressure on the other team when we get the upper hand. Being behind only makes Pat watch himself more."

The Heisman Trophy presentation in 1971 had not yet become the media extravaganza it is today. Contenders weren't invited to New York. Whereas Bo Jackson was present in person when the announcement was made that he had won, in 1971 Sullivan watched the event on television with his wife, his parents, and close friends at the Heart of Auburn Motel.

To this day, Sullivan's teammates say that he was the ultimate team player and leader. When he missed a day of Gator Bowl practice in 1970 to accept the SEC Player of the Year Award in Nashville, he apologized to all his teammates:

"You all read the papers and you know where I was. I'm sorry I had to go during practice, but I want you to know I didn't accept the award for me, I accepted it for you. Any praise or credit I get doesn't belong to me, it belongs to you, and I thank you for letting me be your representative."

As the 1971 season unfolded, Auburn, Alabama, Georgia, Oklahoma, and Nebraska established themselves as contenders for the national championship. Sullivan, who as a junior had finished sixth in the Heisman balloting, now was the leading contender for the trophy.

Ralph "Shug" Jordan, Sullivan's coach and friend, called him "the most complete quarterback I've ever seen. When he's in the game, there's not one thing your offense is not capable of doing."

Alabama coach Paul "Bear" Bryant added his Sullivan vote: "He does more to beat you than any quarterback I've ever seen."

As the season progressed, Sullivan felt mounting pressure to win and to deal with the Heisman hype. Sports information director Buddy Davidson became a friend and confidant.

Sullivan, back home in Birmingham in 2002 as offensive coordinator at UAB, said, "There were a lot of distractions. Buddy did a great job of keeping everything organized. People talked as much about the Heisman as they did our season. Every day there was some kind of media thing. It really wore on me."

Just as Jackson would do fourteen years later, Sullivan stepped to the front against Georgia in Athens. By any measure, it was as big a game as Auburn had ever played—the latest in a season that two unbeaten SEC teams had met. The atmosphere was electric.

"The hype of the game and the atmosphere were unbelievable," Sullivan recounted. "We rode the bus over, and twenty or thirty miles outside of town (Athens) the Georgia students met us and started circling the buses. They were shouting things, throwing beer cans, all kinds of stuff. Once that all started, you could've heard a pin drop on the bus."

Georgia students kept it up at the Auburn team hotel, circling the building in cars, honking horns until early in the morning.

Sullivan's answer to all this: he completed fourteen of twenty-four passes for 248 yards and four touchdowns. Auburn won 35–20 to set up an even bigger game against unbeaten Alabama.

But first there was the Heisman. It was a two-man contest between Sullivan and Cornell running back Ed Marinaro. The announcement would come Thanksgiving night at halftime of the Oklahoma-Nebraska game. When the big moment finally arrived, Sullivan was announced as the Heisman winner.

Pat accepted the news as he had everything else, with calm and grace. His teammates and Auburn students celebrated wildly. Two days later, Auburn's dream of a national championship died in a 31–7 loss to Alabama, to this day an unhappy memory for Auburn players who were there. Sullivan believes Auburn lost its emotional edge when the Heisman winner was announced.

A month later, Auburn lost to Oklahoma 41–22 in the Sugar Bowl.

"I'm not saying we would have beaten Alabama," Sullivan said, "but our senior class had never lost to them. We didn't play very well."

Long before he got to Auburn, Sullivan had displayed the leadership skills that would serve him so well. He excelled in football and baseball. When he was twelve, he saw his first Auburn football game. He sold cold drinks at Birmingham's Legion Field as Auburn beat Georgia Tech 17–14.

Pat went to John Carroll, a Catholic high school in Birmingham. His exploits there for a team short on talent and numbers won considerable attention. After Carroll lost a road game at powerful Huntsville (Alabama) High School, Huntsville coach Tom Owen commented, "Gentlemen, you just saw the finest quarterback ever to set foot on this field."

Sullivan was the first player chosen in the second round of the NFL draft. He played four seasons with the Atlanta Falcons, then briefly with the San Francisco 49ers and Washington Redskins.

After a successful effort in the insurance business, in 1985 Sullivan went into coaching as a Pat Dye assistant at Auburn. Later he became

Pat Sullivan of Auburn, winner of the 1971 Heisman Trophy. (Courtesy Auburn University)

head coach at Texas Christian University. At this writing (2002) he was offensive coordinator at UAB.

Brother Joe and son Patrick followed him as Auburn quarterbacks.

For many of those who were there, Sullivan always will be the epitome of an Auburn football player. He played with courage, grace, and class.

Today's Auburn players see those Heisman Trophies. They see the pictures, hear the stories, and perhaps dream of one day being on that stage.

Twenty years after he won the Heisman, Sullivan was in New York to be honored again. He was one of fifteen players and coaches inducted into the National Football Foundation Hall of Fame. The other inductees chose Sullivan to speak for them.

Pat told the crowd at the Waldorf-Astoria Hotel on December 11, 1991: "It is a special honor and privilege and special responsibility for me to stand before you on behalf of the inductees. It is a responsibility I do not take lightly. None of us started out years ago with thoughts of making the Hall of Fame. For us to stand before you is an honor, but also a humbling experience. To know that our names and exploits will be recorded alongside those who have gone before us is a humbling experience.

"All of us are here tonight to renew our commitment to give something back to the game that has given so much to each of us."

It was vintage Pat Sullivan.

22

Alabama's Compleat Tennist

WENDELL GIVENS

IN RETROSPECT, WADE HERREN ARRIVED on the Birmingham and Alabama tennis scene on cue, right off a tennis pro's script. Perhaps the cue and script references call for a tad of imagination from readers.

In the summer of 1941, a fellow named Martin Buxby, after an impressive tennis record at the University of Texas, came to Birmingham to serve as tennis professional at both the Birmingham Country Club and the Mountain Brook Club. After college, Miami-born Buxby had climbed in national rankings before accepting the invitation to Birmingham.

Birmingham News columnist James Saxon Childers interviewed Buxby on tennis generally and Birmingham tennis specifically. Summing up, Buxby told Childers that what Birmingham urgently needed was a really great player who could excite the city with his tennis skill and, in so doing, heighten interest in the game itself.

That year, fourteen-year-old Wade Herren was developing into one of the genuinely talented tennis players in Alabama. The very next year (as if on cue from Buxby) he brought home the state's first-ever national tennis championship. In time Herren became much the news-making tennis figure Buxby had described to Childers—hence the seeming prophecy fulfillment.

The fact is, Herren's lifelong participation in and devotion to all things tennis perhaps have surpassed Buxby's vision. He has competed successfully for more than half a century, played some of the giants in the game, tutored free clinics, operated a first-class tennis shop, designed and built courts, invented clay court maintenance equipment now in use throughout the nation, founded and edited a regional tennis magazine, served in tennis administration, promoted countless tournaments and tennis celebrity visits, and in yet other ways helped raise the level and quality of tennis in Alabama.

Birmingham News tennis columnist Ronald Weathers once called Herren "Mr. Tennis" in Alabama because of his multifaceted career. Weathers recently told me, "He still is." Time now to turn back some pages in Herren's career.

A Southside youngster, Wade was playing baseball at a neighborhood park one 1930s day when older brother Wood summoned him to forget baseball for the moment and join him at tennis, a new game for the younger brother. Wade didn't question his brother's summons; after all, Wood was big brother who called the shots on what the Herren boys would do on a given day.

Right away, Wade found tennis to be even more fun than baseball. After several weeks on the court with Wood and others, he knew for certain he had found his game.

Wood, who played on the Ramsay High School tennis team and was runner-up in state high school singles his last year, coached and encouraged Wade, and soon the tall, slender youngster was winning most of his pickup matches. He played at every opportunity and, with Wood as tutor, steadily improved his strokes.

The brothers often practiced in the yard of their Southside home, with Wade always assigned the low side of the court so he would chase balls that frequently rolled downhill.

Alabama's "Mr. Tennis," Wade Herren, in action. (Wade Herren
Collection)

Wade entered (and often won) local tournaments and soon was
looking for stiffer challenges. So in 1942, with the encouragement
of a new friend, junior player Jack Tuero of New Orleans, Wade entered and won the Southern Boys (fifteen and under) Tournament at
Clinton, South Carolina, where he defeated Billy Smith of Orlando,
Florida, 6–1 in the third and deciding set.

On down the road that year was the National Boys Tournament at
Culver, Indiana, and Wade, again encouraged by Tuero, decided to en-

ter. His game plan was to constantly hit deep to wear down opponents, and that strategy worked well at Culver.

Thanks largely to Jack Tuero's encouragement, Herren played confidently through to the final, where his opponent was talented Tom Molloy of Memphis. Herren prevailed 8–6, 6–3 and proudly took home Alabama's first-ever national tennis championship. Trophy in hand, he climbed into the baggage area of a Greyhound bus for the happy trip home.

In the fall of 1943 the Herren brothers lost their father, who drowned on a fishing trip. Wade said his mother's strong religious faith helped pull the family through the tragedy.

As a Ramsay High senior Herren again proved he was the best high school player in Alabama by winning the state singles championship a second straight year.

After graduation he served two years in the Navy, which temporarily put a halt to his tennis career, but his court skills had caught the attention of Tulane University in New Orleans, a Southeastern Conference school. Tulane awarded him a varsity tennis scholarship, and there he became a teammate of friend and confidence builder Jack Tuero.

Competing in the strong SEC further sharpened Herren's tennis, and in only his sophomore season he won the coveted SEC singles championship, defeating Georgia Tech's Ed Adams in the final 6–4, 9–7, 6–4.

For his last two years of college, Herren decided to stay home and attend Birmingham-Southern College. Tennis was strong at BSC, and Herren's presence made it even stronger. Years after his play there, he was inducted into BSC's Tennis Hall of Fame.

Now with military service and college behind him, the young man with so much tennis talent had come to a crossroads—actually, two crossroads. At the first step, a soap-opera author might have sized him up: *Wade Herren Faces Life*.

The young man had to go to work, had to earn a living. After some cogitation he tried the insurance field, but he soon acknowledged that

Herren (*far right*) was a star on the 1948 Tulane tennis team. Others (*from left*): Jack Tuero, Dick Moledous, Les Longshore, Harcourt Waters. (Courtesy Tulane University)

insurance definitely was not the right field for him. Not surprisingly, he turned to tennis. But a more critical intersection lay ahead.

Herren realized that for many years he had been concerned about only one person, Wade Herren, and about one thing, pleasure—as in good times. He decided to take a self-inventory. What he found, he said, was a totally self-centered life headed nowhere and producing few worthwhile results.

So what was he to do? Where was he to go? Wade said: "At that point I got on my knees and prayed to God for divine guidance. I asked God to take over my life and to lead me to whatever worthwhile career I should follow, and how I might meet a special someone to love and cherish as my wife."

He said he got the requested assistance on all three needs.

First, he stopped acting on the "self first" principle and began trying to help others, starting at church.

Second, through an arrangement with the Birmingham Park Board, he took charge of the tennis courts at Highland Park and there ultimately changed the face of tennis in Birmingham.

Third, he was introduced to and soon began courting a young Englishwoman, Vivien Mary Stretton Smith, who was teaching at the Birmingham Conservatory of Music. Vivien, too, was fond of tennis, and soon she became fond of Wade as well. Down the road they became Mr. and Mrs.

After Wade took charge of Highland Park tennis, he changed from player alone to player/tutor/consultant/builder/inventor/editor.

Long ago, English author Izaak Walton, who was absorbed in everything related to fishing, produced a book titled *The Compleat Angler*. With that title in mind, we could fittingly call Wade Herren *The Compleat Tennist*. (In some dictionaries, *tennist* is a synonym for tennis player, Birmingham librarian Jim Pate told me.)

Because this book is primarily about athletes and teams, Herren's impressive role as a tennis *merchant* will be capsuled. It is included because what Herren did when he put his racquet aside greatly enhanced his overall contribution to tennis and helped to create the image Martin Buxby had described as necessary if Birmingham hoped to gain the attention of the tennis world.

Herren's agreement when he took over at Highland Park included holding free tennis clinics so that Birmingham newcomers to the game could learn the basics. There's no way to measure the lifetime of pleasure he made possible for countless rookies.

The clinics were only the beginning. Herren founded the Highland Racquet Club, which drew top players from across Jefferson County. According to *World Tennis* magazine, the Highland tennis facility under Herren's supervision was among the top ten in the nation after he put the existing clay courts in top condition and supervised construction of six new ones.

Herren raised the tennis shop's design and inventory so that it became a national model. He began getting requests for maintaining courts and for building others from scratch. With no available specifications, thus at first largely through trial and error, he ultimately built nearly a thousand courts. He also modified and invented maintenance equipment that helped put courts in excellent condition.

He developed the nation's first automatic court sprinkler system and devised a system called the Court Coordinator to manage the flow of people who came to play.

Herren also saw the need for a regional tennis magazine. As none was on the market, he created his own. He found a place to work, then wrote and laid out his own material. Then he found a printing shop that would publish *Southern Tennis.*

All the while he continued to compete. And win. In 1951 he entered the National Public Parks Tournament at St. Louis, where the defending champion and a host of other skilled players waited to take on challengers.

Herren worked his way to the semifinals, where his opponent was defending champion Clyde Hippenstiel of California. When Hippenstiel won the first two sets and took a 2–0 lead in the third, the outcome appeared dark indeed for the young man from Birmingham.

Then, as game three of the third set began, Herren heard a strong, clear call from nearby: "C'mon, Stick, let's get going!" The familiar voice of friend and occasional opponent Jack Chapman of Birmingham seemed to fire up Herren, he told me. Perhaps also hearing the hometown nickname "Stick" (because of his slender build) somehow added to his determination. From then on, Herren took charge of the match.

He rallied strongly to win the third set, then maintained the momentum through the fourth and fifth sets to oust the defending champion 3–6, 1–6, 6–2, 8–6, 6–0 and enter the title round. There he made fairly quick work of George Stewart of St. Louis in straight sets—6–3, 7–5, 6–1—and headed back to Alabama with his second national championship.

In later years Herren would win two national doubles titles, one teaming with Gus Palafox and the other with Tom Bartlett. He also earned No. 1 ranking in Alabama and the South several times.

Then there are Vivien and the children—Wood, Patrick, and Bridget—all active and title-winning players.

After graduating from the Royal College of Music in London, Vivien had come to America to teach at the Birmingham Conservatory of Music. She telephoned Wade about scheduling court time at Highland; they met and chatted, and soon a relationship developed. When Vivien once mentioned returning to England, Wade talked her out of it and later into marrying him.

In 1967 Wade and Vivien won the Southern husband-and-wife doubles.

In earlier years Herren had matched strokes with some of the giants of tennis, such as Pancho Gonzalez, a powerhouse player who usually had his way with opponents; Atlanta's Bitsy Grant, who despite being small played with a big heart; and Cincinnati's Tony Trabert, who on a given day could outdo almost any opponent.

Herren recalled a match with Gonzalez when they were 4–4 in the first set. If he could win two more games, he'd have the strong man down a set. Pancho was serving at love–40, Herren thus a point from breaking. "Then Pancho aced me, moved over and aced me again, then forced me into an error," Herren remembered. "That made it deuce, and Pancho served two more aces. When he needed a point or points, he had his way." The second set also went to 4–4, and then Pancho again stepped up the pressure and won.

In his heyday, Georgia's Bitsy Grant was a marvelous player who could compete with the best. But as he aged, fatigue began to get him, Herren said. Once they were waging a hot match in a Southern tournament at Memphis. In the third and deciding set, Herren noticed that Bitsy—twenty years older—was finding ways to stall, such as going after a ball and kicking it "accidentally" to gain a few more seconds of rest, or perhaps toweling off frequently. Other players watching the match began to chuckle at Bitsy's stalling.

Herren, too, was suffering from the hundred-degree heat, but he finally told Bitsy, "Come on, let's play."

"He was a great guy who put on a great show, and we were good friends. But I knew he was hard-pressed to continue. Finally he looked at me and said, 'I apologize, but I can't go on.'"

So Herren won the match by default, then lost in the semifinals to Gus Palafox.

Onetime West End High star Marvin Buchanan, who served four years as president of the Alabama Tennis Association, recalled seeing Herren take on Trabert at the Birmingham Country Club. As mentioned earlier, Herren's forte was hitting deep forehands that eventually wore down opponents. But on that day, Wade's favorite weapon was turned against him.

"Wade would start a point from the baseline," Buchanan recalled, "then often wind up near the backstop as Trabert pounded away and moved to the net—the man was so strong." Herren agreed.

So what did a former two-time national singles champion do after six decades of working at tennis, on and off the court—that is, in addition to operating Herren's, his tennis business? As of this writing, Wade still plays occasionally, at a less hectic pace, but still with great enjoyment, especially when he joins in family tennis. With Vivien as partner, he competes in mixed doubles, and the two watch with pride when their three children take to the court. (The compleat tennis family!)

Birmingham's Mr. Tennis still finds ways to encourage others to benefit from tennis. He compiled and published twenty-five reasons a person should play tennis, including for physical, mental, and spiritual benefits.

Herren remembers, in addition to his satisfying triumphs, the time he took self-inventory and asked God to change his life's direction. He often shares that memory with fellow members at Briarwood Presbyterian Church and with others throughout his world of tennis.

23

Iron Man in the Making

WENDELL GIVENS

WHEN SEWANEE, THE UNIVERSITY OF the South, paused in October 1999 to salute its football Iron Men of a century earlier, the *New York Times* took note with this page-width headline: "Greatest college team ever? Untouchable, forgotten Sewanee."

High praise for a newspaper customarily sparing with superlatives.

Take a bow, Alabama. The captain and star ball carrier of that 1899 "greatest ever" team grew up in Montgomery and after his Sewanee years was a Birmingham business executive and civic-minded citizen.

The pioneer-years football star was Henry Goldthwaite "Diddy" Seibels, elected to the Alabama Sports Hall of Fame and the College Football Hall of Fame.

Seibels's exploits at Sewanee were chronicled, first by the Sewanee campus newspaper and yearbook, over the decades since by sports columnists across the nation, and in the 1992 book *Ninety-Nine Iron,* a detailed account of the never-matched 1899 Sewanee season.

In recent years Hollywood has nibbled at the idea of portraying the 1899 Iron Men in a movie.

Diddy Seibels's boyhood years in Montgomery helped develop him for his role as leader of Sewanee's Iron Men. The iron in Diddy Seibels surfaced early in life.

As described in a sister-in-law's biography of her husband and Diddy's brother, Temple, the four Seibels brothers (there was one sister) were scrappy, adventurous, and athletic. They fought with their classmates, explored underground rain sewers, and on occasion teamed up (all except Diddy, the youngest) to pull a plow breaking ground for a family garden. The home acreage on South Perry Street covered a full block. While young, the four brothers shared one bed, a huge one. Their quilt was made of worn-out pants they'd outgrown.

The following excerpt from Fanny Marks Seibels's biography of Temple, a noted Montgomery solicitor, capsules Diddy and his three older brothers.

> The Seibels boys were rough members of society. They belonged to a clan, consisting of Arringtons, Goldthwaites and Seibelses, all descendants of Judge George Goldthwaite who was Alabama's first senator to the United States Congress after the Civil War. The members of the clan did not hesitate to jump over a fence if tempted by the sight of ripe watermelons or a tree burdened with red apples; they engaged in bloody fights at school; they swam in the Alabama River, which was dangerous because of swift undercurrents. Evidence points to the fact that they were not law-biding citizens, for one day Dolf Gerald (chief of police) came to the Seibels home and asked to speak to Miss Annie Laura. Dolf Gerald said, "Miss Annie Laurie, I am sorry to have to tell you this. I've got your boys. I had to pick them up." She thought a minute, then answered, "Today is Friday. Mr. Gerald, can't you keep them until Monday?" (Used with family permission.)

If Diddy played prep football while attending Starke's University School, a few blocks from his home, this researcher could find no record of it. But for certain, and on record, he loved baseball (and later golf) and played at every opportunity. His skills, especially as a pitcher, attracted the attention of a Montgomery semipro team, and he incurred his mother's displeasure by touring with the team. The tension eased when his mother learned that professional baseball paid well.

Older brother Temple had preceded Diddy at Starke's and had played football at Sewanee. Undoubtedly that helped stir the younger brother's interest in the still-new game.

Diddy enrolled at Sewanee in 1896, went out for football, and immediately attracted attention with his speed afoot and his love of solid physical contact. He became starting right halfback as a freshman and performed impressively as Sewanee won three games and lost three. One of the wins was over Alabama.

In 1897 the Sewanee record fell to 1-3-1, including a scoreless tie with Auburn. Then, in 1898, Diddy and his teammates posted four straight victories before the season was cut short by a scare of yellow fever.

With several experienced players returning, prospects for the 1899 season were already bright. Then the new student manager, Luke Lea, helped push Sewanee football to heights never dreamed.

Member of a prominent Nashville family, Lea had become a big man on campus soon after enrolling. He was a mover and shaker, the center of attention whenever possible. Early on he wanted Sewanee to reach for football glory, and by his senior year he rolled the dice.

Lea had maneuvered his way into becoming student manager, in those years a position much like today's athletic directors.

First, he brought in Billy Suter, a former Princeton star, as head coach. Then, noting Sewanee's need of an experienced quarterback, he recruited William "Warbler" Wilson of Rock Hill, South Carolina. Wilson had played a year of football at the University of South Carolina before working in his father's law office.

Further, when Sewanee's designated 1899 football captain left school, Diddy Seibels was chosen to replace him in that leadership role. Perhaps Lea had had a hand in that, also.

Growing up in Montgomery, Diddy Seibels played
baseball, then later was a star pitcher at Sewanee.
(Courtesy University of the South)

So, all the pieces were in place for a banner year, and with Montgomery's Diddy Seibels as star ball carrier, talented punter, and defensive standout, it happened.

Sewanee opened the 1899 season with a double-header weekend
triumph in Atlanta. On Saturday, Seibels scored a first-half touch-

down as Sewanee defeated Georgia 12–0. Sunday was for resting, then Monday the Tigers from Tennessee whipped Georgia Tech 32–0. All Diddy did against Tech was score four of his team's six touchdowns.

Back home at Sewanee the next Saturday, Diddy had a field day, running for three touchdowns as Sewanee walloped Tennessee 46–0 despite playing in heavy rain. Southwestern Presbyterian of Clarksville was next to fall, 54–0, as Diddy starred once again, running for three touchdowns.

Meanwhile, Lea had been lining up what would become known as the "Texas trip" for the Sewanee team—an unheard-of five road games in six days, all with major universities: Texas, Texas A&M, Tulane, Louisiana State, and Ole Miss.

Students of football history know the results of that suicidal schedule—five road victories against major opponents, most after difficult overnight train rides. Perhaps most astonishing, Sewanee did not allow those five opponents a point, not even a field goal.

Another point worth remembering is that rules in that day included this one: a player who left a game for any reason, even injury, could not return to play.

Because of that rule, Captain Seibels had preached to the squad of only twenty-one players before they left Sewanee, "Don't get hurt!" One guess as to the first player to be hurt!

The twenty-one players, coach, trainer, and student manager made the twenty-five-hundred-mile trip by chartered Pullman sleeper. To head off risk from possibly harmful drinking water on the extended trip, they carried a barrel of their own spring water from Sewanee Mountain. They also carried textbooks to keep abreast on studies.

Montgomery's Diddy Seibels is the focus of this chapter, hence most of the material relates to him, but recognition of the other members of the Sewanee travel squad is in order. Coach Suter, Lea, and trainer ("rubdown man," they called him) Cal Burrows rounded out the party.

First-stringers were William "Warbler" Wilson, quarterback (blocking back and signal caller); Ormond Simkins (Seibels called him the team's best player), fullback; Ringland "Rex" Fisher of Bridgeport, Alabama, left halfback; Bartlet Sims and Bunny Pearce, ends; John William Jones and Richard Bolling, tackles; Henry Keyes and William Claiborne, guards; and William Henry Poole, center.

Substitutes who made the trip were Ralph Peters Black, Preston Brooks Jr., Harris Cope (who later coached at Howard College), Andrew Evins, Daniel Hull, Joseph Kirby-Smith, Landon Mason, Floy Parker, Albert Davidson, and Charles Gray.

Sewanee's first stop on that historic trip was Austin, Texas, on Thursday, November 10. Sewanee had beaten Texas the previous year and won again 12–0. As mentioned earlier, Seibels had admonished his teammates not to get hurt, then was the first to be injured. He suffered a gash on his forehead and "bled like a hog," an Austin paper reported. But he was quickly bandaged and played on admirably, scoring both Sewanee touchdowns.

After an overnight train ride to Houston, Seibels again played well as Sewanee defeated Texas A&M 10–0. Another overnight ride in their private Pullman took the squad to New Orleans for a Saturday clash with Tulane that Sewanee won handily 23–0.

The Tennessee travelers got their only day of rest on Sunday, then boarded their car for Baton Rouge, where, on Monday, Seibels ran for two touchdowns as Sewanee romped 34–0. At Memphis on Tuesday, Diddy scored a first-half touchdown as Sewanee won a hard-fought struggle with Ole Miss 12–0.

After a rousing welcome home and a week's rest, the Iron Men romped over Cumberland 71–0 and looked ahead to meeting Auburn, coached by John Heisman, in Montgomery the following week. Diddy Seibels played before home folks, including his family, but Auburn gave Sewanee all it could handle.

At Oak Park, on a field used also for professional baseball, the two teams collided in a rowdy, boisterous struggle. Auburn scored first, but Sewanee fought back and held an 11–10 lead at halftime. Because of constant delays and wrangling, darkness came on, cutting the second half short with Sewanee hanging on to win 11–10.

Diddy Seibels and his teammates played one more game that memorable 1899 season, against North Carolina in Atlanta. Reportedly it was a "challenge" for the college football championship of the South.

Rex Kilpatrick kicked a field goal that won the game for Sewanee 5-0, but an Atlanta newspaper reported that Seibels's "wonderful punting" was the game's highlight and that he made the bulk of his team's gains.

After graduation, Seibels served a year as headmaster of Sewanee Grammar School, which later became Sewanee Military Academy. Then he moved to Birmingham, where he and Sewanee friend Robert S. Jemison Jr. established an insurance and real estate partnership.

Long an avid golfer, Diddy won the Alabama amateur championship in 1922.

He and his wife had two sons, Henry G. "Buzz" Seibels Jr. and H. Kelly Seibels, both of Birmingham, and two daughters, Mrs. Laetitia Frothingham of New Canaan, Connecticut, and Mrs. Anne Heroy of Birmingham.

Diddy died in 1967 at age 91.

It is noteworthy that 104 years after their father performed his Iron-Man feat at Sewanee, the sons were still active in Birmingham businesses.

24

The "Marne Football Battles"

Wendell Givens

Did someone say "war"? Obviously someone did, as the headline reproduced on the next page shouts. But rather than a shooting war, the headline referred to a long-ago football game between Howard and Birmingham-Southern College, an annual clash called the "Battle of the Marne," a name borrowed from a fierce battle in World War I.

The king-size headline appeared in Birmingham-Southern's campus newspaper, the *Hilltop News*. The headline and the accompanying story were aimed at helping inspire Southern's football Panthers to defeat the archrival Howard Bulldogs in the Marne finale in November 1939. The Howard-Southern series, lasting from 1906 to 1939, is capsuled here as a "grand" sports memory for Alabamians. The recounting recalls random highlights and heroes of the crosstown rivalry.

I was able to contact a sampling of Panthers and Bulldogs who participated in the Marne battles. They agreed that the Howard-Southern game was always the season's highlight for both schools, the make-or-break event. At least for alumni, players, and students, the

Southern's *Hilltop News* cheered on the Panthers with this headline before the final "Battle of the Marne." (Courtesy Birmingham Southern College)

Battle of the Marne was similar to today's Alabama-Auburn Iron Bowls.

Howard fullback/quarterback Joe Gann, who had played high school ball at Jones Valley, minced no words in recalling the ferocity of the Marne games. "Records up to that point didn't matter," he said. "On game day it was dog eat dog, all-out but clean." Gann recalled that once he blocked a Panther defender, "caught him on my shoulder, carried him toward the Southern bench and told him, 'OK, buddy, this is where you get off' and dropped him there."

Ed Cooper, mid-1930s Southern tackle from Anniston, said he still carried a scar from knocking heads with the Bulldogs. "In those days we didn't have the face guards provided today, so almost everybody lost a tooth or two. Well, *one* of our guys didn't, a boxer/football player who always kept his boxing mouthpiece handy." Despite the determined hitting, Cooper said he couldn't remember even one Bulldog-Panther fight breaking out. Cooper participated in Southern's rousing 21–20 victory in 1937 after two straight losses to Howard.

Paul Davis, Howard '37 and a sturdy guard from Cherokee, was described in Howard's *Entre Nous* yearbook as "making the middle of the Bulldog line a rock wall." Davis proved that in Howard's upset of Ole Miss at Oxford and again in Howard's prized 7–7 tie with Alabama in 1935. One of his favorite memories is of Pete Ellis winning a game for Howard with a long touchdown punt return. In post-Howard years Davis became good friends with former Southern end Woodrow Bratcher. "He never let me forget the field goal he kicked to beat us 21–20," Davis remembered.

Herbert Acton and Roy Malone, Birmingham-Southern student managers, shared memories of their behind-the-scenes participation: taking care of equipment, bandaging ankles, and helping arrange travel for road games. Acton, 1934 manager, recalled that season's Panthers as "a good team comprised largely of good old Sand Mountain boys." Southern defeated Auburn 7–0 and walloped Howard 21–0 during what may have been the Panthers' finest season ever.

Malone was manager for two years, 1935 and 1936, and although

DAVIS AND BANCROFT

H O W A R D ' S

A TRIBUTE TO THE COACHES

Strong-willed arbiters of athletic justice, great-minded sponsors of great sports, these professors hold sway over the kingdom of the gymnasium. Gentlemen in both word and deed, these men have set a high standard for their students. They demand cleanliness on the campus and on the athletic field and both possess the force to put their wishes into deeds. Both sons of Howard, they return to restore glory to her name.

142

Billy Bancroft played, then coached at Howard. (Courtesy Samford University)

Howard won both years, he relished his close-up role with the Panthers. He remembered Coach Jenks Gillem, who had learned the art of drop-kicking while at Sewanee, demonstrating to Panther players how to drop-kick field goals and extra points. Instead of kicking a ball from placement, as is done today, a player dropped the ball, end down, directly in front of him and kicked it the instant it hit, directly toward the goalposts.

The Howard-Southern rivalry was enhanced with what the movies called "added attractions." The extras included parades of competing student-built floats, pranks, and rival student campus raids that were mostly clean fun but occasionally turned ugly. And in the 1920s a "raid" turned tragic when a student was slain.

Apparently, soon after the football rivalry began in 1906, students raided the crosstown campus (Howard in East Lake, Southern on the Westside) and made off with prized mementoes or with student captives whose heads often were shaved.

Bulldog Paul Davis recalled leaving a downtown Birmingham movie house with comrades and suddenly being pelted with rocks from presumed Southern supporters. Chances are, Howard supporters retaliated in kind.

Jimmy Tarrant, Howard freshman in 1939, recalled helping trap a carload of Hilltop defenders. A freshman football group that included Tarrant drove to the Hilltop and began taunting students there. As the Bulldog raiders had hoped, a carload of Southern students chased them off campus and back toward Legion Field. At the stadium, another carload from Howard, having hidden there earlier, emerged and surrounded the pursuit car. Just as a battle royal was shaping, Tarrant recalled, a police car drove up and headed off a possibly bloody fight.

The student fatality referred to earlier occurred on November 21, 1928, when—according to news accounts—a Southern student appeared at a Southside pharmacy to "get" a Howard student employed there. The employee, defending himself with a pistol, fatally wounded the visitor. The Howard student later was cleared of a manslaughter charge.

The shooting apparently halted the worst of the hell-raising, but pranks continued until the football rivalry ended with the 1939 game.

Game week brought all-out preparations for rival parades featuring student-built floats that often required around-the-clock decorating the night before. To those worker bees, winning "best in parade" ranked close to winning the ball game.

This sampling from the *Hilltop News* illustrates the point: "Remember those nights-before-the-game when we hammered and glued on a float-in-the-making until the next day's parade seemed an impossible dream? . . . The thrill at seeing the float—our ideas—next morning, strange but beautiful . . . Southern's parade days are over, but memories go on forever."

And this quotation from a Howard student after the farewell 1939 game, which Southern won: "Lamentations . . . the joy of our heart is ceased; our dance has turned into mourning . . . the crown has fallen from our head; woe unto us."

Game-week memories stayed with Birmingham-Southern alumnus Bob Luckie: "No question, the Southern-Howard rivalry was big; to me, as big as Auburn-Alabama later. But the social week also was big. We dressed up for the November game wearing topcoats, ties and, some of us, hats.

"I remember a pre-game Thanksgiving dinner when Mrs. White, our KA housemother, had prepared a grand dinner table with the customary baked turkey as centerpiece. But before we sat down, Billy Moore, a pre-med student, had someone distract Mrs. White while he slipped in a formaldehyde cat to replace the turkey. It smelled up the place and caused turmoil, but after a while things settled down, the turkey was restored, and we did our best to forgive Billy Moore. Later we considered it all a part of game-week fun."

During the Battle of the Marne years, a surprise development was the transition of Howard head coach Jenks Gillem to Southern head coach Jenks Gillem. It came about this way: Gillem, who had played college football at Sewanee, entered coaching ranks at old Owenton College, a forerunner of Birmingham College. After World War I he joined Head Coach Charlie Brown at Southern as assistant.

Then in 1924 Gillem moved to Howard as an assistant to Harris Cope, who had coached him at Sewanee. When Coach Cope died, Gillem was named head coach at Howard, serving until 1927. Then, when Southern coach Harold "Red" Drew left in 1931 to help coach at Alabama, Gillem went back to the Hilltop as head coach. His last coaching was at Sewanee, his alma mater.

Another Marne-years oddity: in 1917 a promising prospect named D. C. "Peahead" Walker enrolled at Howard and joined the football squad. Little was made of it in those early football years, but Peahead had already played briefly at Southern. Today Walker is best remembered as a colorful and successful coach at Wake Forest College in North Carolina.

A quarter century after Princeton and Rutgers had kicked off college football in America in 1869, the exciting new game had gotten a toehold in the South, at first mostly among larger universities. By the start of the twentieth century, smaller schools were fielding teams. Howard College got aboard in 1902 and Southern (later to be Birmingham-Southern) two or three years later.

Howard and Southern played first in 1906, a practice game at Howard that, in this recounting, is not listed as an official game. The first scheduled game was played in 1907. Technically, the first ten games of the rivalry were between Howard and Birmingham College. Through merger the name became Birmingham-Southern in 1918.

Of the thirty-one games played in the Battle of the Marne rivalry, Howard won thirteen, Southern ten, and eight were ties. In those thirty-one games, six were one-point victories; Howard won five of those.

The rivalry information that follows is thumbnail, gleaned from Birmingham dailies and campus papers and yearbooks. Players' first names were sometimes hard to come by, and sports information departments at Howard and Southern were asked to double-check what is here. Nevertheless, I accept responsibility for what's printed. Thanks to Southern and Howard (now Samford University) for assistance.

1906—Four years after Howard had fielded its first team, Birmingham College (in Owenton) asked for and was granted a practice game at Howard. Someone kept score (51–0 Howard). The practice outcome is not included in total wins and losses in this recounting.

1907—With a weight advantage, Howard won the first scheduled game in the rivalry 87–0 on a muddy field at West End Park, on First Avenue North at Seventh Street. Other than that win, Howard had a poor season.

1908—Surprisingly, this year Birmingham College held Howard to a 12–11 win at West End Park. The Panthers scored first, and Howard needed a safety to win.

1909 at West End—Howard won, 26–0. Birmingham protested that Howard won by playing three "ringers"—ineligibles. Howard's James Williams drop-kicked a field goal, reportedly the first such kicked in the South. A fellow named Wyckham ran a kickoff back for a touchdown.

1910—No Howard-Birmingham game this year; cursory research did not turn up the reason.

1911—The new Rickwood Field baseball park provided a better playing site, and Howard eked out a 6–5 victory. The winning points were the only ones Howard scored in an otherwise poor season.

1912—Birmingham College broke through for its first victory over crosstown Howard, 13–6 at Rickwood.

1913 at Rickwood—Howard won easily 31–0.

1914 at Rickwood—In rain and mud, the teams battled to their first of several ties, 6–6.

1915 at Rickwood—Another 6–6 tie. Kemp Capps ran twenty-five yards for Birmingham's touchdown, then Howard's Campbell tied it. In the second half Howard drove to the one yard line, but Birmingham stopped four attempts to score, saving the tie.

1916 at Rickwood—Birmingham won 15–0. Leading only 2–0 at the half, the Westsiders pulled away with touchdowns by Eddie Lewis and Frank Neill.

1917 at Rickwood—World War I was being waged, and there was no Howard-Birmingham game. D. C. "Peahead" Walker of Ensley, who had played briefly at Birmingham, had joined the Bulldogs.

1918 at Rickwood—Birmingham College and Southern University of Greensboro had merged to become Birmingham-Southern College on a Westside hilltop. The merger helped produce a 26–15 victory. Depleted by flu, Howard later was embarrassed by Marion Institute 101–0.

1919 at Rickwood—Howard scored a safety and hung on 2–0.

1920 at Rickwood—Birmingham-Southern won 14–7. BSC's Maynard Baker scored first on an eighteen-yard pass play, then the Panthers made it 14–0 when Fred "Brin" Brinskelle intercepted a pass and ran it in. "Peahead" Walker saved Howard from being shut out with a nifty touchdown run in the fourth quarter.

1921 at Rickwood—Southern posted its second straight Marne victory, 16–14. The Panthers built a 10–0 lead and held on.

1922 at Rickwood—Howard got back on the plus side, 9–7. The second-half kicking by Ham Stevens enabled Howard to triumph, barely. Southern was lined up on the Howard seven yard line for a winning field-goal attempt when the final whistle blew.

1923 at Rickwood—Another 6–6 tie.

1924 at Rickwood—Yet another tie, this one without a point. Howard head coach Harris Cope had died earlier in the season and was succeeded by Jenks Gillem, who had played under Cope at Sewanee. As taps was played at halftime, Southern students held up a banner bearing the words "In memory of Coach Cope."

1925 at Rickwood—In a hotly contested game, Howard managed a 20–16 victory.

1926 at Rickwood—In their final game played at the baseball park, the rivals fought to a 7–7 tie. Yank Miller ran eighty-seven yards for Southern's touchdown, then Billy Bancroft sparked Howard to the tying score.

1927—Birmingham's new football stadium, Legion Field, awaited the new football season, and who better to play the dedicatory game than Howard and Southern? Before seven thousand fans, the Bulldogs outplayed the Panthers 9–0. Billy Bancroft passed to Sam Spicer for a touchdown, then kicked a field goal to ice the victory. Earlier in the season Howard had played Auburn to a 7–7 tie. (Through the years, Southern defeated Auburn three times.)

1928—This year and to the end of the Marne series, the games were played at Legion Field. Howard won the 1928 game by a whisker, 13–12. Southern had upset Auburn 6–0 and Howard had lost to Auburn 25–6, yet in the Marne contest the Bulldogs prevailed. Howard's "Soup" Davis recovered a Panther fumble for a touchdown, and a long Russell Bullard run got the Bulldogs another. Southern's two scores came on Billy Smith passes to Shorty Ogle and Chink Lott. The difference: Howard converted an extrapoint try and Southern missed on both points-after.

1929—Howard pulled out another one-point win, 7–6, under new coach Eddie McLane before thirteen thousand. Sam Spicer capped a first-half Bulldog drive scoring from the one-yard line, and Tom Bondurant kicked the telltale extra point. In the second half Norman Pilgreen went eight yards for a Panther touchdown, but a pass attempt for the seventh point fell short. Howard center Ray Davis was credited with superlative line play.

1930—Southern coach Harold "Red" Drew had joined future Alabama coach Frank Thomas at Chattanooga. Former Howard coach Jenks Gillem now directed the Panthers. Howard scored first as Ed Sweeney hit Herman Clark with a forty-yard touchdown pass. Southern won 13–7 on a one-yard plunge by Pilgreen and a Loy Vaughn pass to Charley Rice.

1931—For the third time in four years, Howard won the Marne game by a point, 7–6. Southern's Al Blanton passed to Hubert

"Chesty" Albrooks for a first-half touchdown, but the Panthers failed to convert. In the second half, Howard's Eddie Sweeney hit Roy Fayet for a touchdown, and Tom Bondurant kicked the winner.

1932—One of Southern's finest teams won the Marne 7–0 and with it the Dixie Conference crown. Masten O'Neal connected with a pass to "Chesty" Albrooks, who made it to the Howard eighteen yard line. After two line bucks, O'Neal hit Ed Owens for the touchdown.

1933—Another tie, this one 7–7. Pete Ellis ran eighty yards for Howard's score, and Dan Snell kicked the extra point. Ernie Teel scored for the Panthers from the four-yard line, and Hermit "Urm" Davis's kick tied it.

1934—Former freshman coach Billy Bancroft was now acting head coach for Howard; Clyde "Shorty" Propst later was named to the job. Earlier, Howard had beaten Ole Miss 7–6 at Oxford, but this day belonged to the Panthers, 21–0. Hermit Davis scored two touchdowns and kicked all three points-after. Ernie Teel scored the third Southern touchdown. Bryce McKay's punting was a large plus for the Panthers.

1935—Billy Bancroft had been named Howard head coach. His Bulldogs had surprised Alabama at Tuscaloosa with a 7–7 tie and had upset Mississippi State, so the Bulldogs were rolling. They defeated Southern 7–0 on Ewing Harbin's touchdown pass to Dan Snell to cap a long drive. Howard's Norman "Shorty" Cooper later was named Little All-American.

1936—Howard 13, Southern 0. Charley Wilcox passed to "Sis" Hopkins for one Howard touchdown. Raymond Christian, star of the day, scored another on a long run. Christian kicked an extra point and ran up an astonishing 259 yards rushing. With the victory, Howard clinched the Dixie Conference championship.

1937—With eleven thousand fans on hand, Southern won a Marne classic 21–20. Dick McMichael passed to J. T. Aldridge to give Southern a 6–0 lead; the extra-point try missed. George Daugherty ran in a Howard touchdown, and Joe Gann's conversion made it 7–6 Howard. Soon another Daugherty touchdown and Gann kick made it 14–6. Rufus Perry then scored for Southern, but another missed kick left Howard ahead 14–12. Daugherty came back with a third-quarter score to make it 20–12 Howard; their first missed conversion would haunt the Bulldogs. Perry scored a second time to put the Panthers within two points at 20–18. With six minutes left, Woodrow Bratcher kicked a twenty-five-yard field goal that won the cliffhanger for Southern.

1938—This was George Daugherty Day at Legion Field. Howard's superb fullback scored two touchdowns, kicked an extra point, and gained 283 yards in forty-two carries. Howard's Clyde White threw touchdown passes to Captain Herman Hodges and Marvin Crawford to cap off a great 25–0 day for the Bulldogs.

1939—In Southern's farewell to football, about eight thousand fans turned out for the Battle of the Marne finale. George Daugherty gave Howard a 6–0 lead in the first half. Early in the third quarter, Dick McMichael returned a punt seventy-two yards for a tying Panther touchdown, and Gus Noojin's extra point made it 7–6 for Southern. As time ran down late in the fourth quarter, Howard tried passing from its end zone, and the resulting safety nailed the last-game decision for Southern 9–6.

25

The Punt That Wouldn't Come Down

WENDELL GIVENS

FOR ME, WATCHING FROM THE Legion Field press box, the scene was and is frozen in time: a football punted from near the north end zone now still spiraling about press-box high toward the south end zone.

Because the punt, by Ramsay High School sophomore John Baumgartner, was expected to land about midfield, its continuing flight stirred surprise, then astonishment among many of the twenty-eight thousand spectators and in the press box. We were seeing something new: a punt that seemingly wasn't coming down.

Seated close by me were Benny Marshall, sports editor of the *Birmingham Age-Herald,* and Alf Van Hoose of the *Birmingham News* sports staff. My job was to write a game feature for the *Age-Herald* on that 1947 Crippled Children's Clinic event.

Coach Ed Eubank's Ramsay team had lost its regular-season game to Woodlawn 13–6, but because Eubank-coached teams came on strong in November, the Clinic rematch had been rated a toss-up. That rating proved faulty when Ramsay ran up a three-touchdown lead in the first half and went on to win 25–0.

Ramsay's John Baumgartner, who launched the punt. (Courtesy *Birmingham News*)

Woodlawn's chances had been jolted when injury benched star blocker Earl Langner. But now the Colonels had stopped Ramsay at the Ram fifteen, and sophomore halfback John Baumgartner went back to punt. He awaited the snap at about his two-yard line.

John Baumgartner had developed skills as an athlete before he reached Ramsay. Asked about his pre–high school years, he remembered being asked to play on older-age teams because he already was talented and was mature physically beyond his years. Thus when he reached Ramsay he was ready for the varsity.

Assistant Coach Thompson "Mutt" Reynolds, interviewed more than half a century later, described John as a solid, all-around athlete in several sports—football, baseball, basketball, and track.

Because Ramsay was cramped for practice space, the football squad had to make do with an eighty-yard field. Baumgartner was soon punting balls "out of the park"—over the end fence and into the street. That prompted Coach Reynolds's observation on what happened in the Clinic game: "It was almost bound to happen."

Van Hoose noted in his game story for the *News* that, rather than getting an assist from a wind, Baumgartner actually had kicked *against* a light breeze. Asked about that, Reynolds said that the wind resistance gave the punt altitude.

Woodlawn's safety man on the punt was substitute half back Bobby Bowden. He said later that he'd been cautioned by Coach Kenny Morgan, "Whatever you do, don't let him kick it over your head." So young Bowden began backpedaling when he saw the punt coming. Then he backpedaled in haste and finally turned and ran back trying to get under the punt.

Baumgartner's boot finally came to earth at the Woodlawn twenty and still had enough "kick" to bound into the end zone, rolling to within a yard of the back line.

Thus my feature story also had "landed." After double-checking the yardage with Marshall and Van Hoose, I reported in my *Age-Herald* story that the bodacious punt—from foot to end of roll—was 104 yards. It went into the record book (perhaps with an asterisk) as eighty-five yards. The scrimmage line had been the Ramsay fifteen, and the touchback meant it came out to the twenty. Technically it was sixty-five yards, but from foot to end of roll it still was 104 yards.

My feature would have been much better had I hustled to the dressing room and talked with Baumgartner and his coaches. My excuse for not doing so was an early newspaper deadline and the need to then assist with the rest of the sports section.

More than half a century later, when I decided to enlarge Benny's book *20 Grand* to this volume, I sat down with Baumgartner at his cattle farm home in Blount County. After reminiscing about Birmingham Big Five football years, I got to the point. "John, why did that punt against Woodlawn travel so far? What was different from your other punts?"

He pondered briefly, then replied: "All I can tell you is, everything from snap to protection to kick execution went right."

Punter Baumgartner and receiver Bowden (*right*) later became good friends. (Courtesy John Baumgartner III)

"Then you must have put more power into your kick."

"Not that I was aware of."

"When did you know you had unloaded a king-size punt?"

John shrugged. "Well, I began running down the field to help defend against a runback, and I saw an official signaling touchback."

"And what did they say on the bench?"

"Aw, they were hollerin' and beatin' me on the back."

Surprised, huh? With that I shut off on the punt and asked, "Ever run into Bobby Bowden in later years?"

He had. "We met on an airliner, recognized each other, and sat down to reminisce about the Clinic game. We became good friends and remain so. My son Johnny made a good-buddies picture of us, and I had it printed on a calendar. Bobby's something, isn't he?"

He is. So is my memory of the kick that seemingly wouldn't come down.

26

Alabama Knocks Off Miami, Wins National Championship

JIMMY BRYAN

UNIVERSITY OF ALABAMA FOOTBALL FANS by the thousands had transformed New Orleans into a sea of crimson as they spent the final days of 1992 preparing to end thirteen years of agony, watching and waiting for another national championship. Not since Coach Paul Bryant's 12-0 season of 1979 had followed 1978's 11-1 for back-to-back national championships had the Tide brought home No. 1.

Standing in the way now were the Miami Hurricanes, who had more or less assumed Alabama's role as college football's bully team. The swaggering 'Canes had won four national championships in the 1980s and were 8.5-point favorites to defeat the Tide and take another.

Alabama had taken home three national championships in the 1960s and three more in the 1970s, but none in the 1980s. Coach Bryant had retired after the 1982 season and died less than a month later, on January 26, 1983. Since then, Ray Perkins, Bill Curry, and Mike DuBose had failed to take the Tide back to the top.

Now, Bryant player and coaching protégé Gene Stallings was try-

Jubilant Gene Stallings gets victory ride (Courtesy *Birmingham News*)

ing. In this third season he had gathered eleven straight regular-season wins, then swatted away Florida 28–21 in the first Southeastern Conference championship game to go 12-0.

What the underdog Tide needed now was one more victory on a stage that stretched across America. Alabama and Miami, playing in the Superdome in New Orleans, had it all to themselves on ABC. The Tide would do the job, powerfully and stunningly, 34–13.

Before recounting details of that battle for the national championship, a recap of the 1992 season is fitting.

Miami had begun the season as defending national champions. With potential Heisman Trophy candidate Gino Torretta as quarterback, the Hurricanes were ranked No. 1 in the Associated Press sportswriters' preseason poll. Alabama was voted ninth.

Obviously, if the writers knew whereof they voted, Alabama would have little more than a peek at the national championship. Miami was favored to win it all again.

Because I'd covered all of Alabama's regular-season games, and hence was in a position to observe the team's week-to-week progress (or lack of), I was asked to write this recap of the Tide season. It's appropriate perhaps to include my two cents' worth on the Tide's preseason chances of winning the national championship.

Looking back a decade later at the preseason 1992 Tide, I would have set the odds at 100–1. Realistically, virtually no chance.

Few people, even the staunchest Tide supporters, could have expected the team to win its way to the Superdome as No. 2 to challenge No. 1 Miami.

In the early days of putting the team together, Coach Stallings had told Alabama sportswriters that any thoughts of No. 1 were farfetched. "I think we're a year away," he'd said.

I agreed with the coach; I didn't believe a national championship was even a possibility. I knew the team was capable on defense with its monstrous front and its incredible speed in what might be the best secondary in America.

Also, I didn't believe the offense was strong enough, didn't believe that talented but untested quarterback Jay Barker had the goods—at least not yet—to contend for No. 1.

The season that would become one to remember began in the stifling dog days of August, which can be almost unbearable in Tuscaloosa by the Black Warrior River.

As *Birmingham News* man on the scene, I marveled at Eric Curry, John Copeland, James Gregory, Damien Jeffries, Jeremy Nunley, Shannon Brown, and the defensive linemen laboring through the dreaded gassers (wind sprints) with line coach Mike DuBose running with them. Jeff Rouzie put his sterling set of linebackers—Lemanski Hall, Antonio London, Derrick Oden, Michael Rogers, Mario Morris, Will Brown, and others—through sweat-dripping work.

Defensive coordinator Bill "Brother" Oliver was at his scheming best (he would be all season) with George Teague, Sam Shade, Antonio Langham, Chris Donnelly, Tommy Johnson, Eric Turner, and some young ones. Teague, Shade, and Langham later would move on to the NFL.

Mal Moore and backfield coach Woodie McCorvey developed a run-oriented group that Barker conservatively directed and didn't let mistakes get it beat. (Barker would throw for 1,614 yards, a modest seven touchdowns, and nine interceptions.)

Of the run group, Derrick Lassic would run for 904 net yards, darting little Chris Anderson would throw his 175 pounds forward for 573 yards, and fullback Martin Houston would go 457 yards and make hole-opening blocks. Exciting David Palmer, Kevin Lee, and Prince Wimbley were there to catch Barker's offerings along with Curtis Brown out of the backfield.

Palmer, who missed the first three games because of DUI stops, wasn't the return man he'd been as a sophomore, but everybody was aware of his number and presence on the field.

Line coach Jim Fuller may have done his best coaching job. Center Toby Sheils stood in the middle of it with Roosevelt Patterson, George Wilson, Matt Hammond, Jon Stevenson, Steve Buskey, and a bunch of young ones—not a pro prospect among them.

The kicking game held up with freshman Michael Proctor kicking points and Bryne Diehl punting.

Well, Alabama kept its heart beating through some early-season scares after a somewhat routine 25–8 opener with Vanderbilt. Proctor began his freshman year successfully by kicking field goals of forty-six, forty-three, forty-two, and thirty-two yards. Lassic scored on a four-yard run and Rogers with an interception of thirty-six yards. Royce Love got Vandy's touchdown on a five-yard run, and Eric Lewis ran a two-point conversion.

As it usually does, Southern Mississippi hung tough before bowing to the Tide defense, 17–10, at Legion Field. A Crimson curtain restricted the Eagles to lows of twenty-eight yards rushing, twenty-six yards passing, and three first downs. Tommy Johnson carried Diehl's pass seventy-three yards on a fake punt before the Eagles scared Bama fans by cashing an interception return eighteen yards to a touchdown and a fumble recovery into a thirty-three-yard field goal. Anderson's one-yard run and Proctor's extra point brought it back with 10:19 left.

The Tide found its offense in Little Rock to slam Arkansas 38–11, prompting me to report for the *News:* "Two surprise guests showed up at War Memorial Stadium Saturday night: President-frontrunner Bill Clinton and the Alabama offense. Arkansas native Clinton was late getting there but the Tide turned a 28–0 halftime quickie into an easy ride. Barker passed for three touchdowns in the first half to Anderson, Buskey, and Lee, and Lassic and Sherman Williams ran short ones in."

Palmer made his first appearance against Louisiana Tech and put his No. 2 jersey in on a dazzling stage. Proctor field goals of thirty-seven and thirty-five yards were all Bama had to show from Tech gnawing at its ankles before The Deuce got loose for sixty-three yards with a punt with 11:05 left. The first shutout of the season was set at 13–0 and left the Tide ranked at No. 9.

For three weeks Washington pushed Miami down to No. 2, then the Hurricanes reclaimed the top.

Alabama offense joined defense in strangling South Carolina, 48–7, at rainy Homecoming. With Lassic, Williams, and Anderson scoring in the first quarter, it was 38–0 and over at the half. Barker passed to Brown, Craig Harris scored on a run, and Proctor kicked a thirty-eight-yard field goal in the second half. Hamp Green kicked a twenty-four-yard field goal in the third quarter, the Gamecocks denied a shutout when Brandon Bennett scored, then Anderson cashed a thirty-seven-yard run to close it out. Alabama climbed to No. 6.

The mighty defense got back in shutout mode with a 37–0 blanking of Tulane in New Orleans. With Lassic exploding for 188 yards and Anderson 84, the Tide rolled to 435 yards on foot. The score had been only 6–0 at the half on Proctor field goals of forty-two and thirty-seven, then 16–0 on another Proctor goal and a five-yard Lassic touchdown. Two touchdowns by Anderson, one a fifty-seven-yarder, and another by Williams in the fourth made it more presentable. Bama moved up to an impressive No. 4.

Now came the third Saturday in October and Tennessee at Knoxville. The Tide held on 17–10, built on two one-yard Lassic touchdowns and a thirty-three-yard Proctor field goal. The Vols got a forty-four-yard John Rocksvoort field goal in the third and a touchdown on a short Heath Shuler pass to David Horn in the fourth to make it nervous, but Donnelly intercepted a Shuler pass with 1:08 left to close the door. The Tide stayed No. 4 in the Associated Press's Top 25; Miami reclaimed No. 1 for the remainder of the season.

Alabama came home and took care of Ole Miss, 31–10. The Rebels insisted on stopping the run, and Barker responded with a career passing day of twenty-five of thirty-nine for 285 yards. Palmer scored on a twenty-two-yard pass, Lassic on a two-yard run, and Proctor kicked a twenty-eight-yard field goal in the second quarter to offset Russ Show's fifty-three-yard pass to Eddie Small. After a scoreless third, Williams went over twice in the fourth and the Rebs added a thirty-two-yard Brian Lee field goal. The Tide remained No. 4.

At LSU the following week the Tide running game came back for 301 yards as Bama romped and jumped to No. 2. When Pedro Sanchez kicked a thirty-five-yard field goal, the Tide trailed for only the second time that season. Proctor matched the kick from the twenty-nine and Lassic got over from the one to make it 10–3 and a lead that would hold up. Barker was sacked in the end zone for 10–5 after a quarter. Anderson's two-yard run sent it to 17–5. Williams for Alabama and Robert Toomer matched third-quarter touchdowns to send it to 24–11, then Williams scored from the twenty-four in the last quarter to round it up. The Tide stayed No. 2 behind Miami.

Alabama rode out a scare at Mississippi State before winning 30–21. Lassic scored on a twenty-three-yard Barker pass, then Langham blocked a punt and returned five yards for a 14–0 lead. Proctor field goals of forty-one and twenty-one doubled State's first field goal points, and it was 20–3 at the half. State slashed through for eighteen unanswered points in the third quarter, but Bama rallied for ten points in the last quarter to make the result look easier than it was.

That set the stage for the Iron Bowl at Legion Field, which stunningly became Pat Dye's final game as Auburn coach. He had shocked the football world by announcing it the evening before. Alabama doubled the misery by handing a Dye-coached team a first shutout. My lead in the *News* read: "The University of Alabama's second-ranked team proved conclusively Thanksgiving afternoon that great talent is a more powerful fuel than emotion. The Tide peeled away the emotion of Pat Dye's shocking resignation to punish the Tigers, 17–0."

Bama didn't peel away the emotion until the second half. The fired-up Tigers held the No. 2 team in the nation scoreless through the first half. Langham's sixty-one-yard interception return in the third quarter relieved the anxiety, and Proctor's forty-seven-yard field goal pretty much put it away. Williams's fifteen-yard run with 12:08 left did for sure.

That sent the Tide into the first-ever SEC championship game with Eastern Division winner Florida at Legion Field. The Tiders would hold back the Gators in a magnificent game worthy of its name.

Langham was the hero one more time. His interception of a Shane Matthews pass and twenty-seven-yard return provided the touchdown that broke a 21–21 standoff and sent the Tide on its way to New Orleans.

The Gators had scored first on Errict Rhett's five-yard pass from Matthews. The Tide came straight back on Lassic's three-yard run for 7–7 after one quarter. Bama went up 14–7 at the half on Barker's thirty-yard pass to Curtis Brown, then moved on to 21–7 on Lassic's fifteen-yard touchdown run. Matthews passed four yards to Willie Jackson to make it 21–14 after three. Rhett's one-yard run tied the score at 21, and overtime appeared a possibility until Langham's heroics decided the issue.

Now the unbelievers of early autumn, including this writer, gradually had become full-fledged believers. And why not? Gene Stallings's Tide stalwarts had plowed through a challenging field of twelve opponents, ten from the Southeastern Conference. Among the vanquished were Tennessee in Knoxville, Auburn in the Iron Bowl, and Florida in the SEC championship game.

Next up would be the swaggering but admittedly powerful Miami Hurricanes with the national championship as prize.

Could the Tide make Miami its thirteenth victim? Not according to the oddsmakers, who made Alabama an 8.5-point underdog. Not according to the 'Canes, who constantly thumbed their noses at Tide players and fans, first on Bourbon Street, then on the playing field.

It had been crazy all week in the French Quarter. As expected, Tide fans and 'Canes fans had been jawing back and forth; that was expected. But Miami players, determined to live up to their reputation as thugs, got into some pushing and shoving. The loudest 'Cane was Rohan Marley, smallish linebacker, who crowed, "We're going out to kick a——. We came here No. 1 and we're going to beat Alabama."

Tide players for the most part kept their cool. Said Antonio Langham, "It's hard to take, but once the game starts, I'll have something to say when I run by him for a touchdown."

Stallings had put 145 players on the travel squad, and not one broke curfew. Most were going to their rooms two or three hours ahead of 11 P.M.

Stallings would recall: "The team was ready when we got to New Orleans. I didn't have to give them a pep talk. I just had to make sure they didn't play the game on Wednesday or Thursday."

Each player was in his own world in the Superdome dressing room before going before the 76,879 who filled every seat. Said Barker: "It was so quiet you could hear a pin drop. It was never like that before. It's never been like that."

Lassic, who would win MVP honors, remembered: "No one had to say a thing. We knew what we had to do. We had to play the game of our life." And they did.

In a few minutes the much-heralded national championship game kicked off before the noisy full house, and Miami's football world quickly began turning upside down.

The Hurricanes had Heisman Trophy winner Gino Torretta at quarterback, but the supposedly best player in college football was about as effective in the national title game as his bronze trophy itself would have been under center. A brilliant defensive scheme from defensive coordinator Bill "Brother" Oliver put Torretta in a coma.

Tide's George Teague at full throttle (Courtesy *Birmingham News*)

Often with eleven men staring him down at the line of scrimmage, he completed only twenty-four of fifty-six passes for 278 yards and no touchdowns, intercepted three times by a secondary that would send three players into pro ball.

If anybody had in mind beating Alabama, it was written in stone: stop the run. Miami knew this but couldn't stop it. Daring, slashing Derrick Lassic frisked college football's eighth-best overall defense for 135 yards and two touchdowns on twenty-eight carries.

The game was tied 3–3 after the first quarter on field goals by Proctor and Miami's Dane Prewitt, an Alabamian from Trussville. The Tide went in front for good with ten second-quarter points. Williams went two yards for the touchdown, and Proctor nailed his second field goal. Prewitt's second field goal finished the 'Canes for the first half.

Alabama had put Miami into a 27–6 hole going to the fourth quarter. Lassic scored from a yard out, and Teague returned an interception thirty-one yards. Kevin Williams got Miami's only touchdown on a seventy-eight-yard punt return in the fourth quarter. Lassic got his second touchdown on a four-yard run to finish the scoring.

En route to the tumultuous upset, the Tide's George Teague made a play for the ages. After an Alabama pass defender slipped and fell, Miami's Lamar Thomas, the team's fastest receiver, caught a pass and appeared headed for an eighty-nine-yard touchdown. Teague, still winded after his own touchdown run, caught the speedier Thomas at the Tide six-yard line, stripped the ball into his own hands, and started the other way. The steal didn't result in a turnover because Alabama had been offside, but it did save a touchdown that Miami never got back.

As Bama player and coach, Bill Oliver had seen brilliant plays in national championship games. He said of Teague's steal, "That may have been the greatest individual effort in Alabama football history."

In the laughing, dancing, singing aftermath, Coach Stallings said, "I never considered us the underdog. I said all along I'd take our team straight up. The coaches had our players superbly prepared. . . . I can't describe how pleased I am in our one hundredth year of football to win thirteen games and a national championship."

WRITER'S GALLERY

CLYDE BOLTON, retired *Birmingham News* sports columnist, was one of the South's first and best-known auto-racing writers. An alumnus of Jacksonville State University, he worked for newspapers in La-Grange, Georgia, Gadsden, and Montgomery before joining Benny Marshall's *Birmingham News* sports staff. He has written several sports books and novels, the latter including *Turn Left on Green,* a stock car racing novel. Bolton is in the Alabama Sportswriters Hall of Fame.

JIMMY BRYAN, Jacksonville State University alumnus, was sports editor of the *Gadsden Times* from 1958 to 1963 and on the *Birmingham News* sports staff from 1963 to 1999. Bryan wrote the "Around Alabama" sports column for the *News* and covered a variety of sports, including Birmingham teams in four professional football leagues, Southeastern Conference athletics, ice hockey, golf, tennis, basketball, and horse racing. He is in the Alabama Sportswriters Hall of Fame.

WENDELL GIVENS, Howard College graduate, worked under Benny Marshall on the *Birmingham Age-Herald* covering high school games, then held *Birmingham News* editing positions. For several years he supervised production of the paper's Sunday football section. He edited Marshall's *Winning Isn't Everything,* a book on Coach Paul Bryant, and Marshall's *20 Grand* sports collection; wrote *Ninety-Nine*

Benny Marshall, sports editor
and author

Iron, an account of Sewanee's five football victories in six days; and co-wrote *Playback* with golfer Elbert Jemison.

PHILLIP MARSHALL, son of Benny Marshall, has covered sports in Alabama for thirty-three years. He has written extensively on Auburn and Alabama varsity athletics for five newspapers, starting at the *Huntsville News.* Later he was assistant sports editor of the *Birmingham Post-Herald,* sports editor of the *Decatur Daily,* sports editor of the *Montgomery Advertiser,* and sports managing editor and college sports editor of the *Huntsville Times.* Currently he covers Auburn athletics for the *Times.*

JIM MARTIN has been *Birmingham News* golf columnist since 1975. He has covered more than one hundred professional golf tournaments, including thirty-seven consecutive Masters tournaments and seven U.S. Opens, including championships by Jerry Pate (1976) and Hubert Green (1977). A Montgomery native, Martin was a golf professional for many years and was golf director at Riverchase Country Club of Birmingham. He was founder and seventeen-time general chairman of the highly successful Charley Boswell Celebrity Classic.

WAYNE MARTIN started writing about sports for the *Birmingham Post-Herald* as a Howard College sophomore. In thirty-three years on the *Birmingham News* he covered everything from high school football to the Super Bowl and the World Series. During most of his career he covered professional baseball. He reported on the Birmingham Barons for twenty-five years and covered major leaguers' spring training in Florida. He visited Atlanta often while the Braves' Hank Aaron chased and broke Babe Ruth's home-run record.

INDEX

Bartholemay, Bill, 138
Bartlett, Tom, 171
Barton, Coker, 68, 71
Batson, Wilton, 93
Battle, Bill, 49
Baumgartner, John, 193–196, *194, 196*
Bean, Andy, 150–151
Beasley, Terry, 156
Beckwith, Bill, 62
Bell, Cool papa, 142
Bell, Peter, 117
Beman, Deane, 134
Bennett, Brandon, 201
Birmingham *Age-Herald*, viii, 92, 195
Birmingham Barons, 1–2
Birmingham Black Barons, 98, 101, 103–104, 142
Birmingham Electric Company, 4
Birmingham *News*, viii, 1, 92, 137, 199; quoted, 45, 51, 61, 201, 203
Birmingham *Post*, 1
Black, Jiggy, 2
Black, Mary Harmon (Bryant), 20
Black, Ralph Peters, 179
Blanton, Al, 190
Boatwright, P. J., 133
Bogan, Jim, 33
Bolling, Frank, 139
Bolling, Milt, 139
Bolling, Richard, 179
Bolton, Charlie, 42
Bond, Florence, 155–156
Bondurant, Tom, 190–191
Bonnett, Neil, 122, 126

Boros, Julius, 25
Boswell, Charley, viii, 111–113, *114,* 115–118
Boswell, Charley, Jr., 117
Boswell, Kitty, 111–113, 118
Bowden, Bobby, 195–196, *196*
Bowman, Steve, 88, 108–110
Branch, Eugene, 129
Bratcher, Woodrow, 183, 192
Brinskelle, Fred "Brin," 189
Brooker, Tommy, 49
Brooks, Preston, 179
Brown, Charlie, 187
Brown, Curtis, 200–201, 203
Brown, Earl, 68, 74
Brown, Jack, 69, 74
Brown, Johnny Mack, 18
Brown, Shannon, 199
Brown, Will, 199
Browne, Herbert, *95,* 96
Bryant, Paul "Bear," vii, viii, 19–21, 46–48, 51–53, 56–57, 59–60, 83–84, 86, 88, 94–95, 106, *107,* 108, 110, 161, 197
Buchanan, Marvin, 173
Bullard, Russell, 190
Burch, Gerald, 48–49
Burger, Tracy, 92
Burkett, Jackie, 40, 42
Burrow, Bob, 35
Burrows, Cal, 178
Bush, Alan, 79
Buskey, Steve, 200–201
Butts, Wally, 11, 13
Buxby, Martin, 165–166, 170
Byrd, Sam, 24, 27, 30

Matthews, Shane, 203
Maughn, Bill, 102–104
Maxwell, Perry, 148
Mayes, T. M., 79
Mays, Willie, viii, 98–99, *100,*
 101–104
McClendon, Charlie, 108
McClurkin, Jim, 13
McCollough, Gaylon, 54, 57, 88
McCorvey, Woodie, 200
McCovey, Willie, 139
McEwen, Tom, vii
McGowen, Jim, 68, 71–72, 74–75
McKay, Bryce, 191
McKenzie, Adrian, 92, 95
McLane, Eddie, 190
McManus, Bayward, 62, 66
McMichael, Dick, 191–192
Meagher, Jack, 11–12, 16
Medwick, Ducky, 3, 6
Mehre, Harry, 18
Melton, Bimbo, 71, 73–74
Middlecoff, Cary, 25, 27–28
Milan, Clyde, 3–4, 7
Miller, Johnny, 130, 151
Miller, Yank, 189
Mills, Don, 63
Mizerany, Mike, 69
Mobile Black Bears, 139, 142
Mogge, Bill, 115
Moledous, Dick, *169*
Molina, Florentino, 149
Molloy, Tom, 168
Montague, Eddie, 104
Moore, Billy, 186
Moore, Mal, 200

Morgan, Kenny, 195
Morris, Mario, 199

Nail, Jimmy, 46
Namath, Joe, 54, 56, 84–90, *85*
Neal, T. V., 91
Neill, Frank, 189
Nelson, Benny, 54, 57
Nelson, Larry, 149
Newbill, Vernon, 109
Nicklaus, Jack, 82, 129, 131, 134–
 135, 149, 154
Ninety-Nine Iron, 174
Nix, Lloyd, 39–45
Noojin, Gus, 192
Noonan, Red, 69, 71
Norton, Jocko, 70
Novick, Joe, 25, 27
Nunley, Jeremy, 199

O'Dell, Richard, 49–52
Oden, Derrick, 199
Ogden, Ray, 87–88
Ogle, Shorty, 190
Oliver, Bill "Brother," 199, 204, 206
O'Neal, Masten, 191
O'Shea, Dennis, 31
O'Sullivan, Pat, 69
Otis, Amos, 139
Ouimet, Francis, 129
Owen, Tom, 162
Owens, Ed, 191

Pace, Toby, 64
Padgett, Don, 151
Palafox, Gus, 171, 173